3-D
BULLETIN BOARDS
With Patterns

3-D

by
Lynn Brisson

Three-Dimensional Bulletin Boards for the whole year

Bulletin Boards with Moving Parts

An Art Activity with Each Bulletin Board

Incentive Publications, Inc.
Nashville, TN

Illustrated by Lynn Brisson
Cover by Susan Eaddy
Edited by Jennifer Goodman and Sally Sharpe

ISBN 0-86530-164-6

TABLE OF CONTENTS

PREFACE

This book is designed to give teachers an exciting new approach to making and using bulletin boards. Now bulletin boards can stimulate learning as well as add color to the classroom!

All of the bulletin boards in this book are three-dimensional or have manipulative parts. Easy-to-follow instructions, actual-size patterns, and finished-product illustrations make these bulletin boards easy to construct and use. By tracing or reproducing the patterns and storing them in your files, you can re-create any board in minutes, again and again!

An easy technique which is used in the construction of patterns throughout the book is a simple cut and fold procedure. This trick gives rounded objects such as fruit or animals a three-dimensional look.

Each bulletin board is based on a theme. Some boards introduce a subject or special unit that the class might be studying, some provide a hands-on skills activity, and others present holiday or seasonal themes in especially creative ways. You'll never be without a bulletin board idea!

Not only are these bulletin boards easy to put together, but they are fun and educational. The class may actually participate in the construction of the bulletin board. Each bulletin board section outlines an art activity which allows the students to make three-dimensional or "free-moving" objects for the board. All you have to do is reproduce the pattern pages, according to the provided instructions, and furnish the materials. Some art activities involve the students even more by engaging them in skills projects or class discussions.

These three-dimensional "learning creations" are sure to motivate every student!

THEME: THE SOLAR SYSTEM

MATERIALS:
- black butcher paper or construction paper
- markers
- glue or tape
- construction paper (assorted colors)
- white chalk
- scissors

CONSTRUCTION:
1. Cover the board with black paper.
2. Trace the sun pattern on yellow construction paper. Glue or tape the sun to the bulletin board as shown.
3. Draw orbit lines around the sun using white chalk.
4. Trace the planet patterns on colored construction paper (as marked). Cut out the planets and glue them on the orbit lines as shown.
5. Reproduce the boy pattern and color it accordingly. Trace the telescope pattern on gray construction paper. Cut out the telescope.
6. Trace the large star pattern on white construction paper. Use a marker to draw a face on the star. Attach the star to the board as shown.
7. Trace the small star pattern on white construction paper. Use a marker to write "The Planets" on the star. Cut out the star and attach it to the board as shown.
8. Attach the boy and the telescope to the board as shown.

ART ACTIVITY:
Have the students make 3-D stars to pin on the board. Give each student a copy of the art activity page and have them make 3-D solar system models.

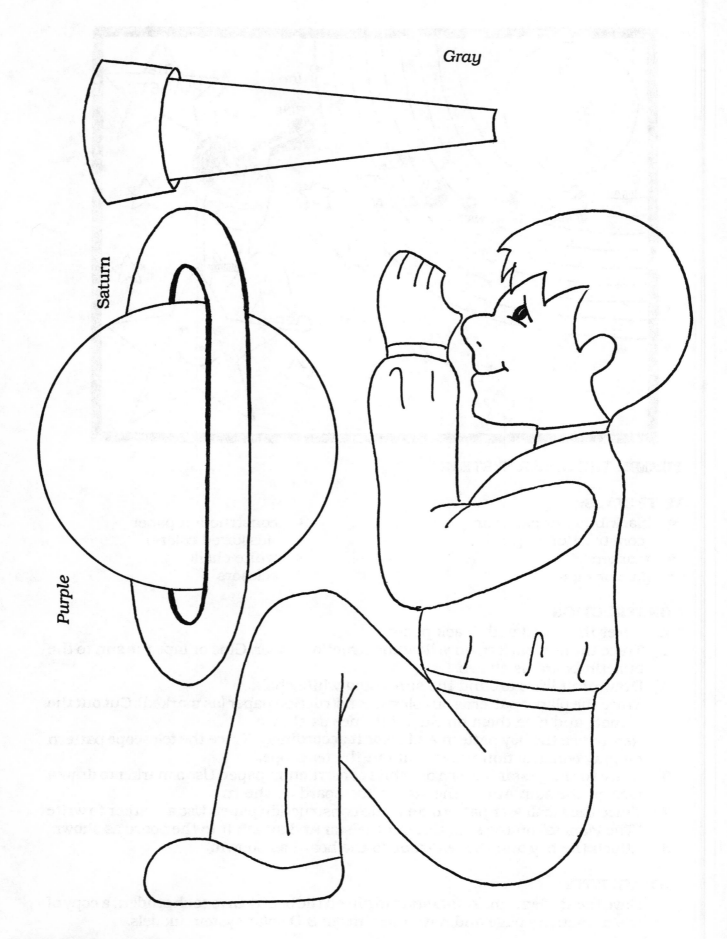

Gray

Saturn

Purple

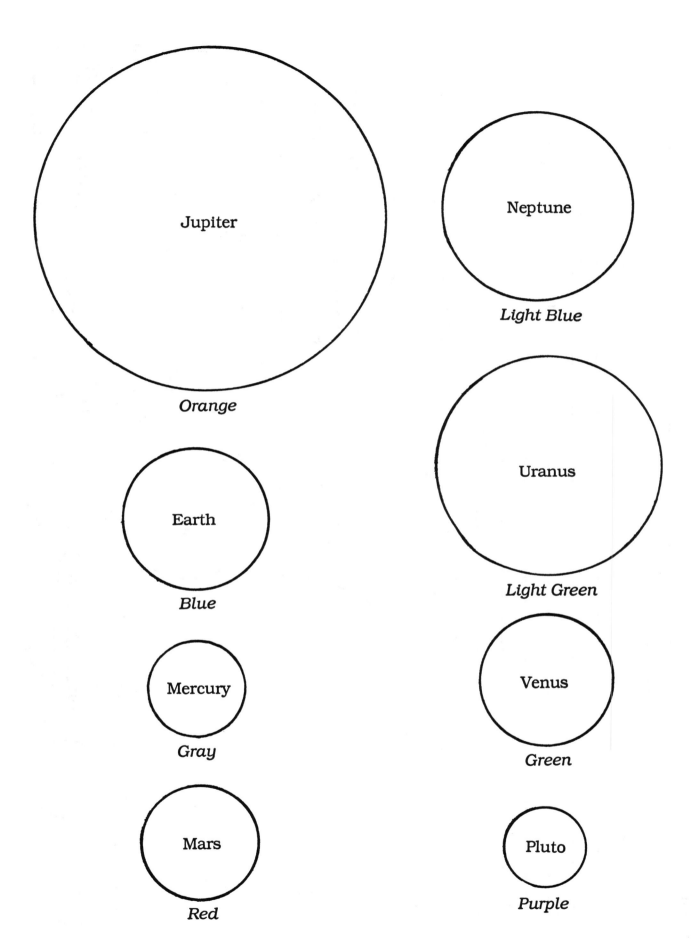

Jupiter

Orange

Neptune

Light Blue

Earth

Blue

Uranus

Light Green

Mercury

Gray

Venus

Green

Mars

Red

Pluto

Purple

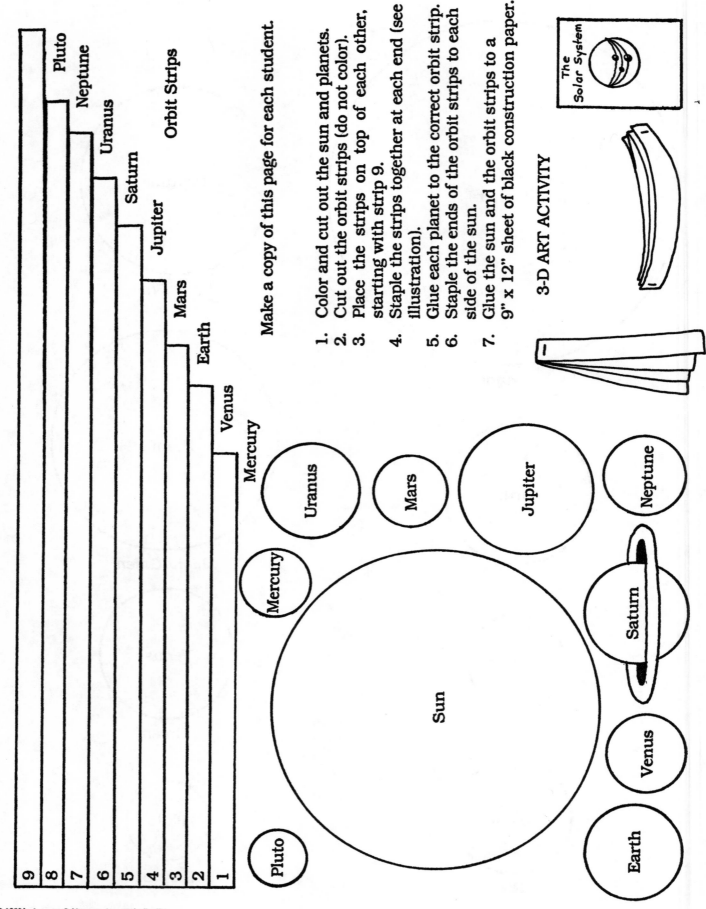

Orbit Strips

9 Pluto
8 Neptune
7 Uranus
6 Saturn
5 Jupiter
4 Mars
3 Earth
2 Venus
1 Mercury

Make a copy of this page for each student.

1. Color and cut out the sun and planets.
2. Cut out the orbit strips (do not color).
3. Place the strips on top of each other, starting with strip 9.
4. Staple the strips together at each end (see illustration).
5. Glue each planet to the correct orbit strip.
6. Staple the ends of the orbit strips to each side of the sun.
7. Glue the sun and the orbit strips to a 9" x 12" sheet of black construction paper.

3-D ART ACTIVITY

The Solar System

Uranus

Mars

Jupiter

Neptune

Mercury

Saturn

Sun

Venus

Pluto

Earth

Place on fold of paper and cut.

Make a copy of this page for each student.

1. Cut 2 stars.
2. Glue the stars together as shown.
3. Fold the points of the top star towards the center. Add glitter to the star to make it "sparkle".
4. Pin the star to the board.

THEME: SEA CREATURES

MATERIALS:
- construction paper (light green, dark green, gray, assorted colors)
- scissors
- crayons and markers
- glue or tape
- blue butcher paper or construction paper

CONSTRUCTION:
1. Cover the board with blue paper.
2. Cut out seaweed from light and dark green construction paper.
3. Cut out rocks from gray construction paper.
4. Use the octopus pattern to trace and cut out a gray construction paper octopus.
5. Glue or tape the seaweed and rocks to the bulletin board. Use markers to draw the top of the water and to label the bulletin board "Creatures of the Sea". (See the illustration.)

ART ACTIVITY:
Discuss the different types of creatures that are found in the sea -- animals with backbones (vertibrates) and animals without backbones (invertibrates). Have each student draw a sea creature for the bulletin board. Using the seashell pattern provided, have each student make a shell for the bulletin board. The shells and octopus are three-dimensional!

13

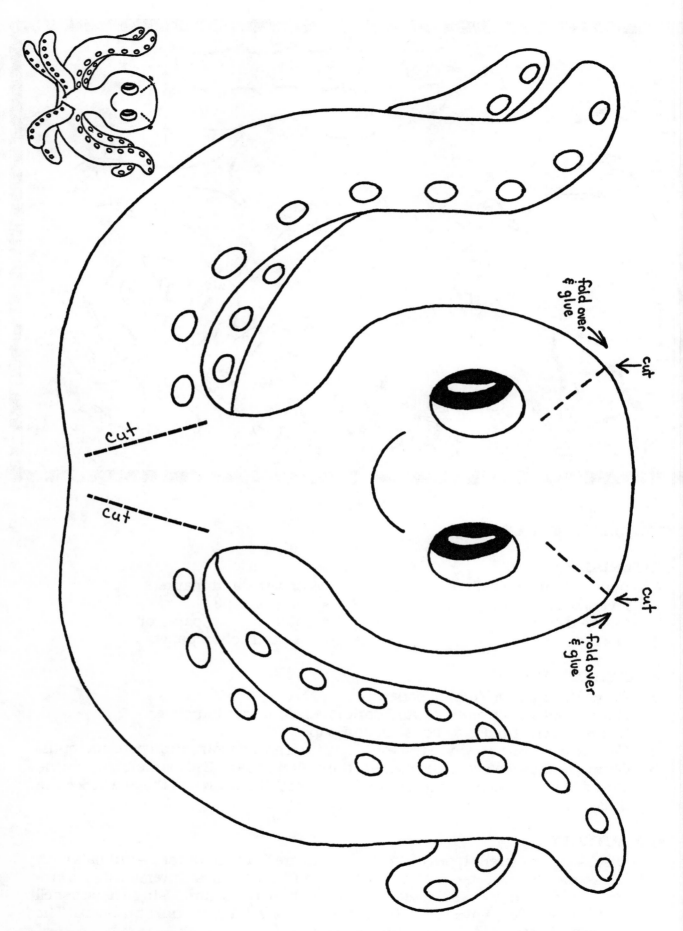

cut

cut

fold over & glue → cut

cut ← fold over & glue

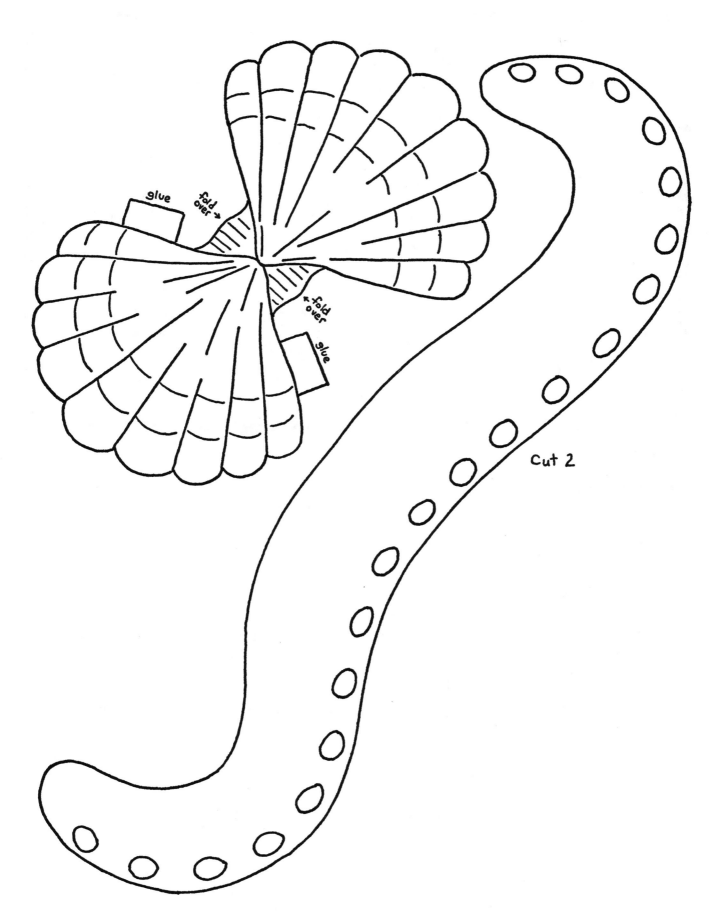

glue

fold over →

← fold over

glue

cut 2

THEME: INSECTS

MATERIALS:

- yellow butcher paper or construction paper
- glue or tape
- scissors
- markers
- construction paper (green, blue, orange)

CONSTRUCTION:

1. Cover the board with yellow paper.
2. Reproduce the insect patterns. Cut out each insect along the dotted lines.
3. Cut a large circle out of blue construction paper and attach it to the board as shown. Using the illustration as a guide, attach the developing stages of the silverfish to the circle. Label the stages and cycle.
4. Cut a large triangle out of green construction paper and attach it to the board as shown. Refer to the illustration to attach the stages of the dragonfly to the triangle. Label the stages and cycle.
5. Cut a large square out of orange construction paper and attach it to the board. Attach the life cycle of the butterfly to the square as shown. Label the stages and cycle.
6. Cut letters out of green construction paper to spell INSECTS and attach the letters to the board.

ART ACTIVITY:

Have each student draw an insect on a jar pattern, label the insect, and cut out the jar. Attach the jars to the board. Discuss the different ways that insects develop.

16

Life Cycle of a Butterfly
Complete Metamorphosis

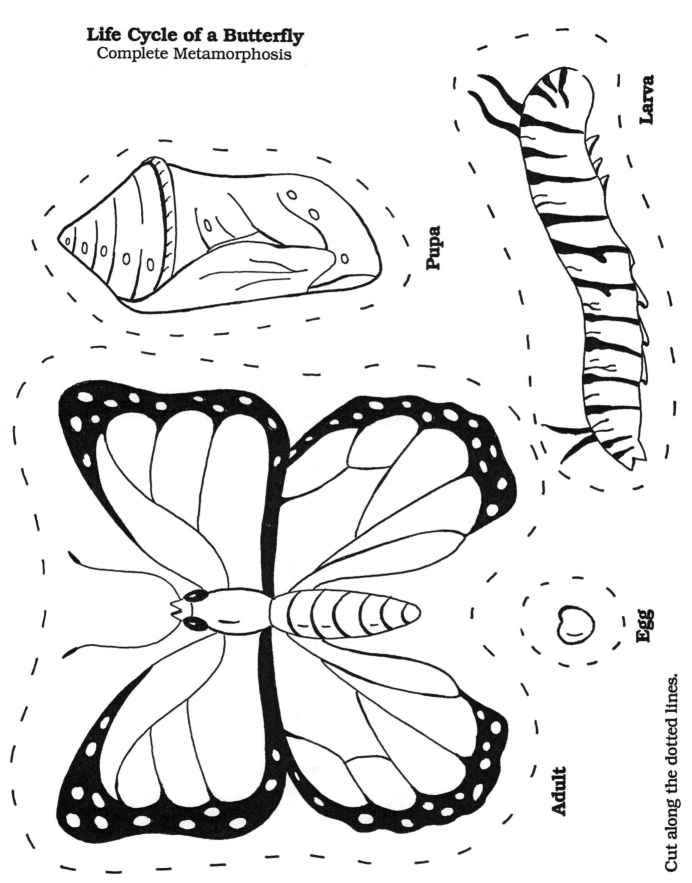

Larva

Pupa

Egg

Adult

Cut along the dotted lines.

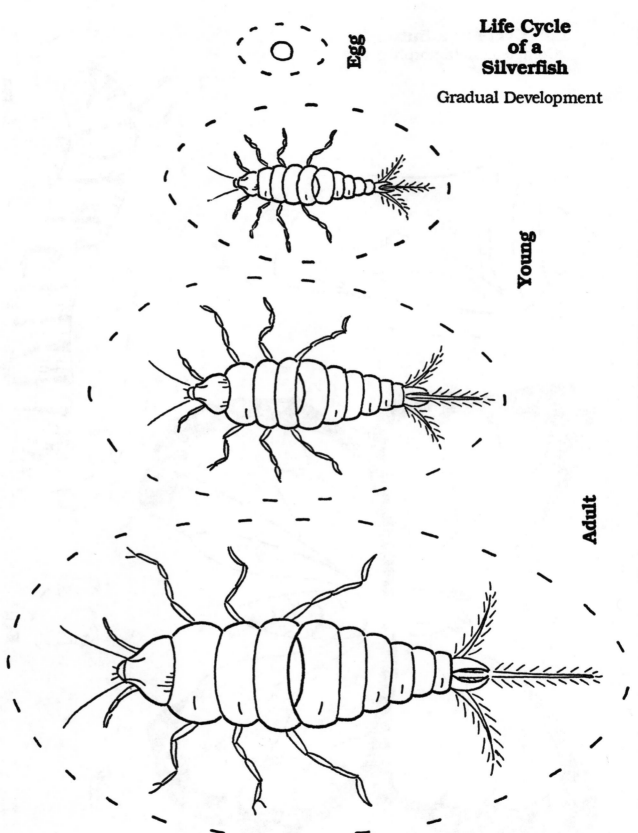

Life Cycle of a Silverfish

Gradual Development

Egg

Young

Adult

Cut along the dotted lines.

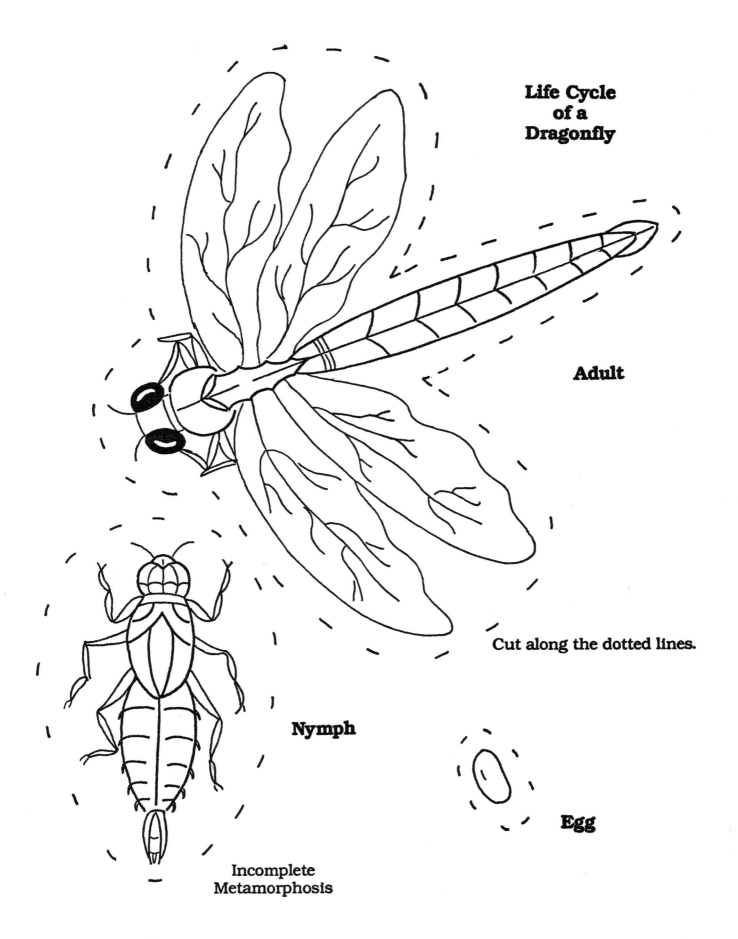

Life Cycle of a Dragonfly

Adult

Cut along the dotted lines.

Nymph

Egg

Incomplete
Metamorphosis

Make a copy of this page for each student.

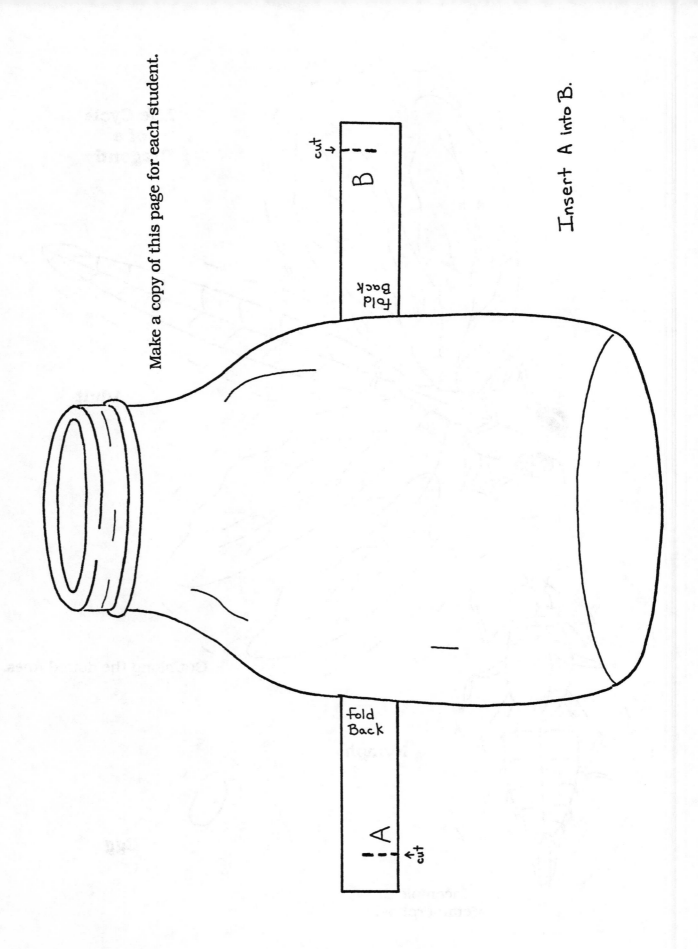

Insert A into B.

cut

B

fold Back

fold Back

A

cut

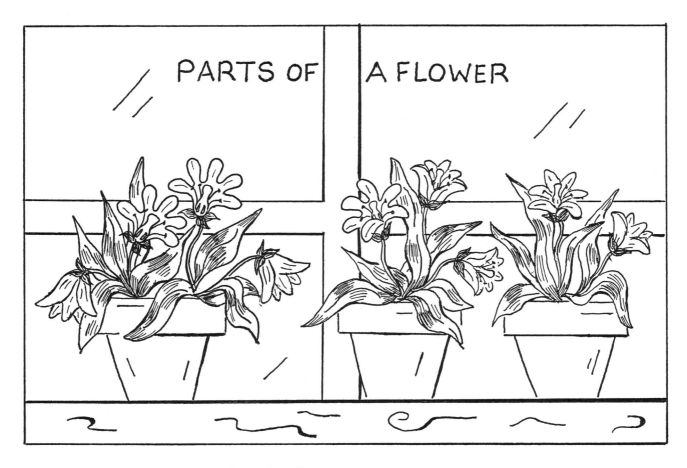

THEME: THE PARTS OF A FLOWER

MATERIALS:
- construction paper (assorted colors)
- glue or tape
- crayons, marker
- pipe cleaners
- yellow butcher paper or construction paper
- scissors

CONSTRUCTION:
1. Cover the board with yellow paper.
2. Cut two long strips from brown construction paper. Glue or tape the strips on the bulletin board to make windowpanes.
3. Cut a wide strip from brown construction paper to make a window ledge. Glue or tape the strip on the bulletin board.
4. Trace the flowerpot pattern on orange construction paper and cut out enough pots to hold flowers made by every student in the class.
5. Glue or tape the flowerpots on the window ledge, leaving the tops of the pots "open". Use a marker to label the bulletin board "PARTS OF A FLOWER".

ART ACTIVITY:
Instruct each student to make a 3-D flower using the patterns provided. Have the students cut out and color each part of the flower. Help the students glue the flower parts together. Direct the students to glue pipe cleaners to the center of their flowers and fold the petals to the dotted lines. Each student should slide a sepal up the pipe cleaner and glue it in place. After gluing leaves to the stems, the students may fill the pots with flowers!

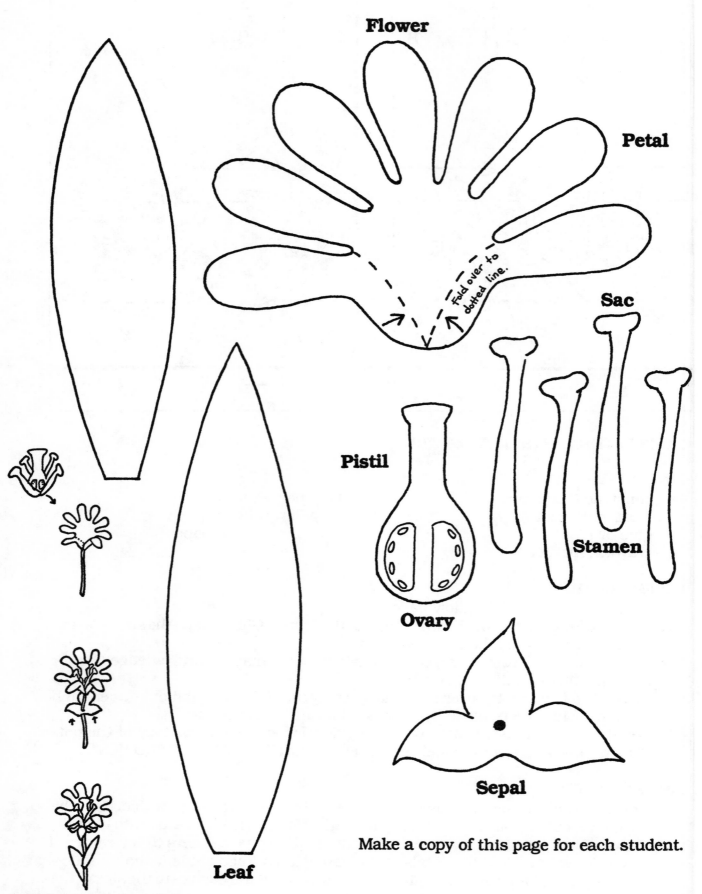

Flower

Petal

Sac

fold over to dotted line.

Pistil

Stamen

Ovary

Leaf

Sepal

Make a copy of this page for each student.

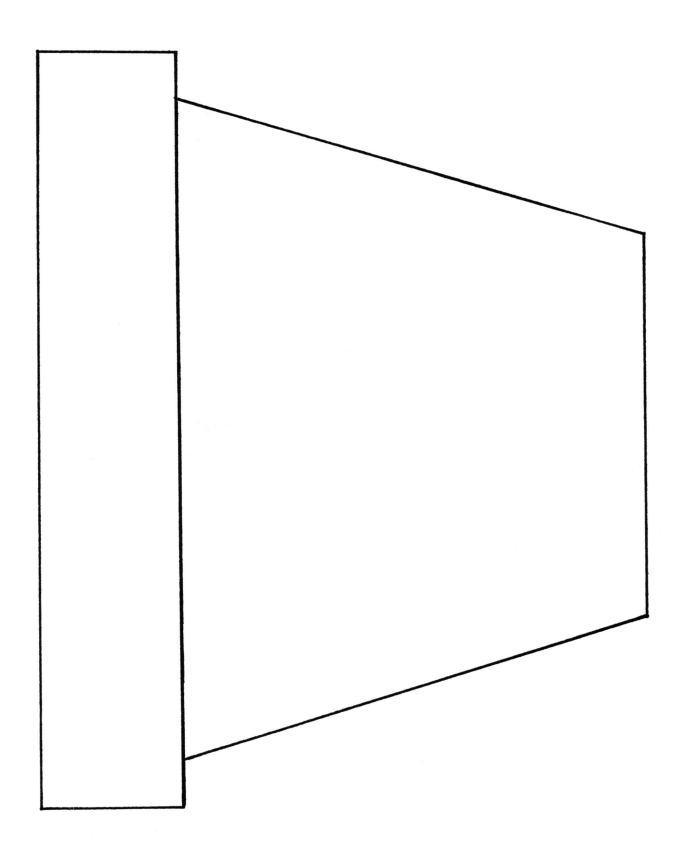

Chef Nutrition is here to say Eat something from each food group every day.

Milk Products
Meat and Poultry
Breads and Cereals
Fruits and Vegetables

THEME: NUTRITION

MATERIALS:

- blue butcher paper or construction paper
- glue or tape
- scissors
- crayons and markers
- construction paper (gray, yellow, fruit and vegetable colors)

CONSTRUCTION:

1. Cover the board with blue paper.
2. Reproduce both patterns for the chef. Cut out the patterns and glue them together. Color the chef's scarf red and his shoes and hair black.
3. Reproduce the cake pattern. Use a bright marker to label each layer with one of the four food groups as shown in the illustration.
4. Trace the platter pattern on gray construction paper. Cut out the platter.
5. Make a sign out of yellow construction paper. Use a marker to write the chef's advice (shown in the illustration) on the sign.
6. Assemble the board as shown.

ART ACTIVITY:

Have the students make funny, 3-D fruit and vegetable faces using the patterns provided. Instruct the students to collect food labels, wrappers, containers, etc. for the other three food groups. Attach the fruits and vegetables and other food items to the bulletin board to make a border. Discuss each food group with the students.

24

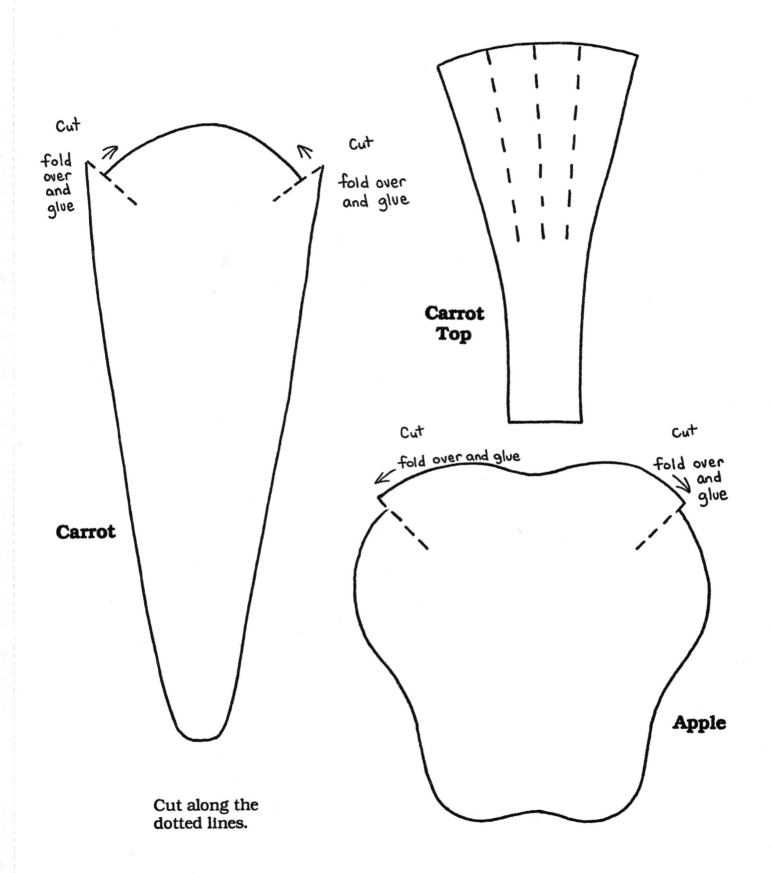

Cut

fold over and glue

Cut

fold over and glue

Carrot Top

Carrot

Cut along the dotted lines.

Cut

fold over and glue

Cut

fold over and glue

Apple

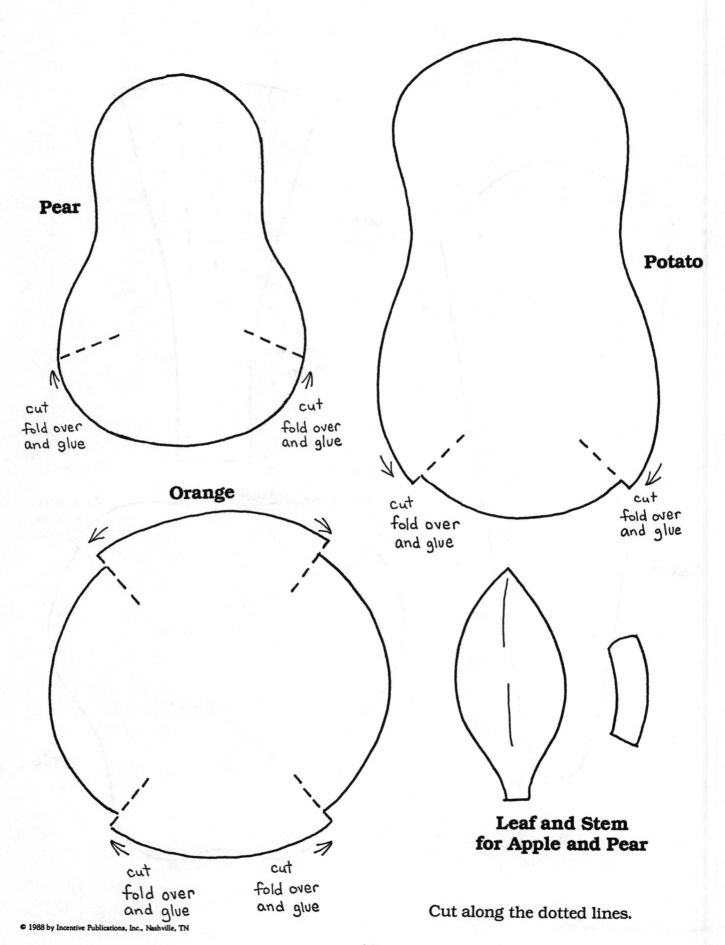

Pear

Potato

cut
fold over
and glue

cut
fold over
and glue

cut
fold over
and glue

cut
fold over
and glue

Orange

cut
fold over
and glue

cut
fold over
and glue

**Leaf and Stem
for Apple and Pear**

Cut along the dotted lines.

THEME: WEATHER

MATERIALS:
- blue butcher paper or construction paper
- scissors
- glue or tape
- crayons
- yarn
- construction paper (white, assorted colors)

CONSTRUCTION:
1. Cover the board with blue paper.
2. Cut clouds out of white construction paper (see illustration). Use a colorful marker to label one cloud "Weather Words". Attach the clouds to the board.

ART ACTIVITY:
Have each student make a colorful "weather" balloon using the pattern and directions provided. Give each student a weather word to define such as dew, snow or fog. Have the student write the word on the basket and the definition on the balloon. Attach the balloons to the board.

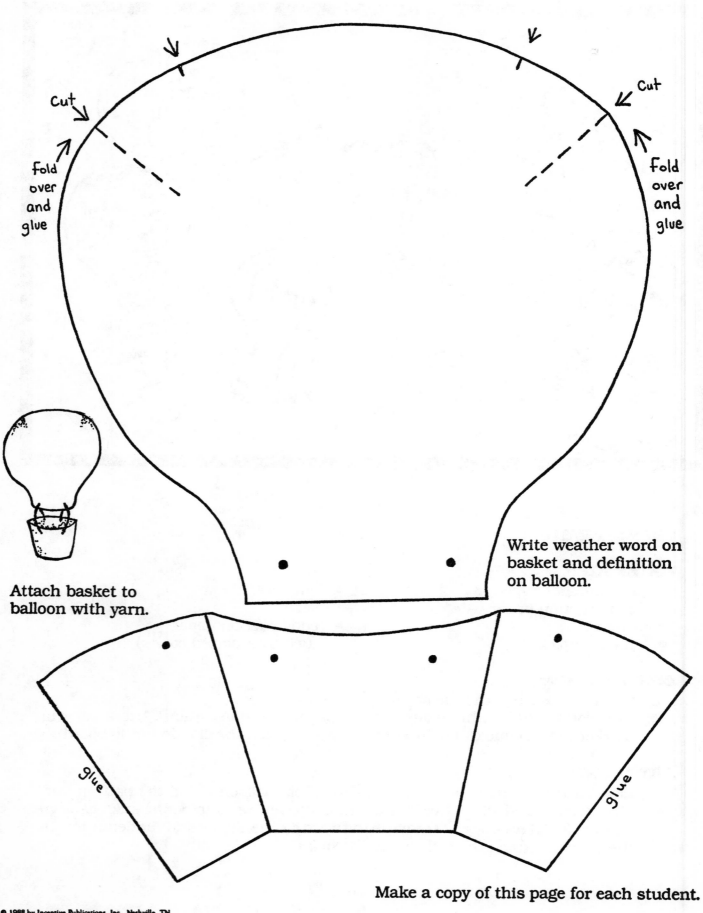

Cut

Cut

Fold over and glue

Fold over and glue

Write weather word on basket and definition on balloon.

Attach basket to balloon with yarn.

glue

glue

Make a copy of this page for each student.

THEME: SPELLING

MATERIALS:
- green butcher paper or construction paper
- glue or tape
- scissors
- construction paper (brown, yellow, white, green, gray)
- markers

CONSTRUCTION:
1. Cover the board with green paper.
2. Trace the mushroom cap pattern twice on yellow construction paper and the mushroom stem pattern (twice) on brown construction paper. Cut out the mushroom parts and glue them together to make two mushrooms. Write the instructions on the mushrooms as shown in the illustration.
3. Cut a wooden post out of brown construction paper. Make a sign using white construction paper and write the weekly spelling list on the sign with a black marker.
4. Trace the body and head patterns for the big snail on gray construction paper. Draw in the details with a marker. Glue the head to the body.
5. Cut grass blades out of green construction paper, curl them on a pencil, and glue them to the board. Assemble the board as shown.

ART ACTIVITY:
Have each student make a small snail using the patterns provided. Pin the snails to the board.

Mushroom Cap

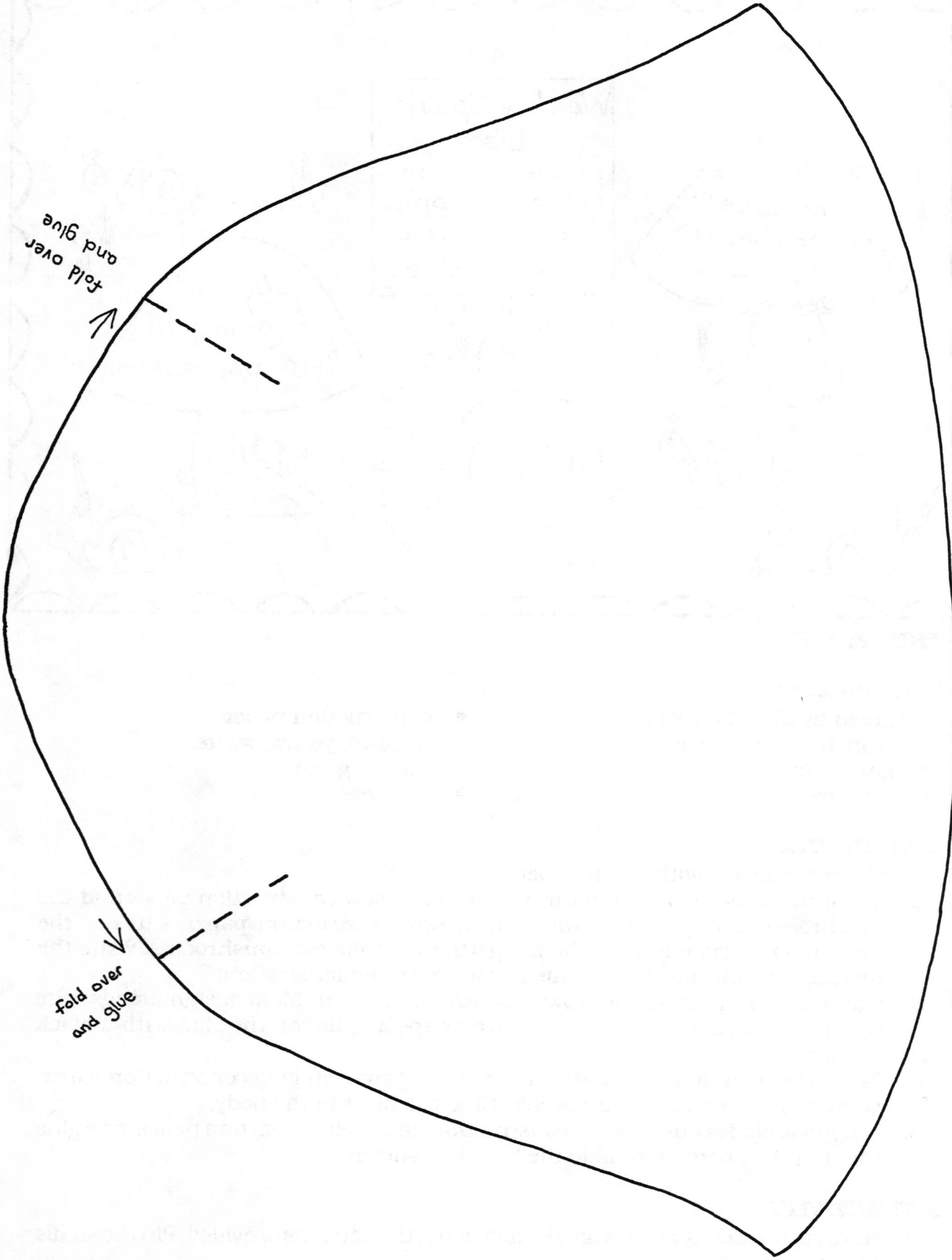

fold over
and glue

fold over
and glue

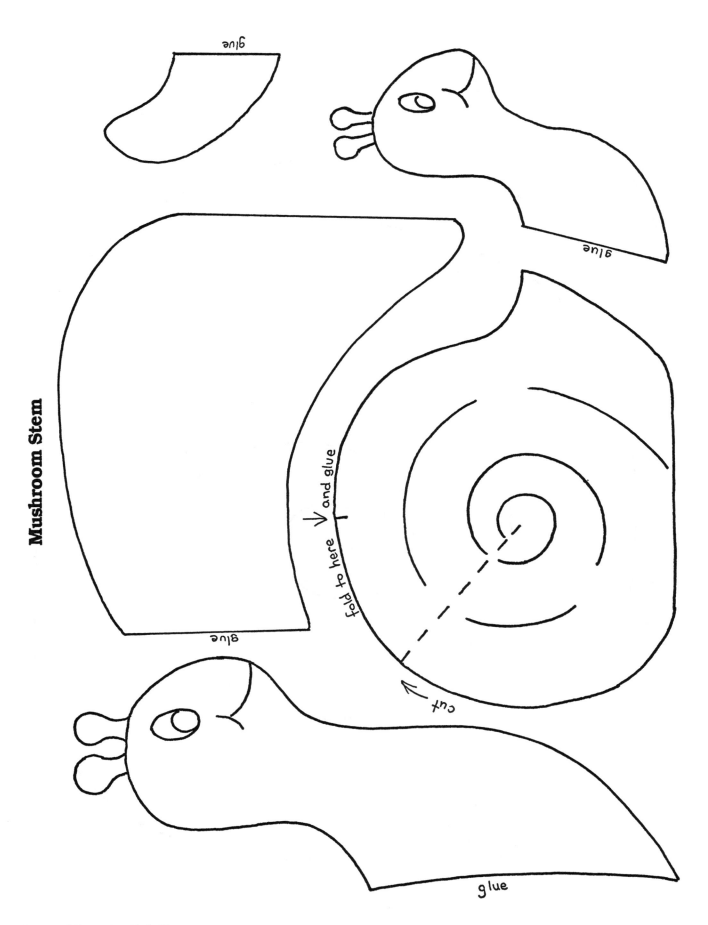

Mushroom Stem

glue

fold to here and glue

cut

glue

glue

glue

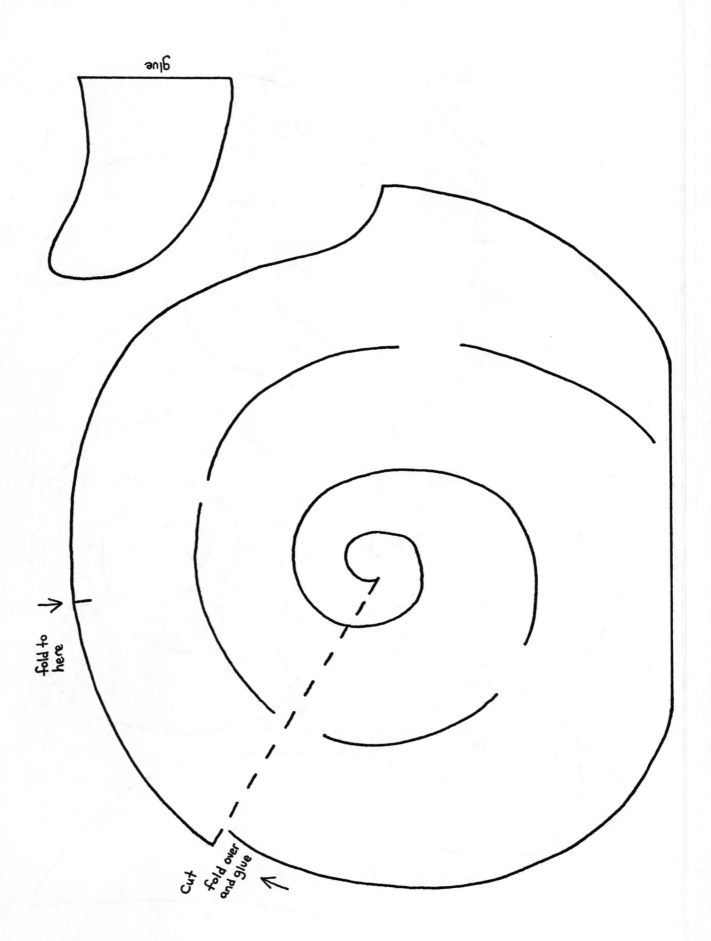

glue

fold to here

Cut

fold over and glue

THEME: PUNCTUATION

MATERIALS:
- yellow butcher paper
  or construction paper
- scissors
- markers
- glue or tape
- white construction paper

CONSTRUCTION:
1. Cover the board with yellow paper.
2. Reproduce all of the pup patterns (head, nose, back, legs, ears) four times each to make four pups. Cut out the pup pieces and color them with a black marker as shown. Glue the pieces together to make four pups.
3. Trace the bowl patterns and cut out four bowls from white construction paper. Use a marker to label each bowl with a punctuation mark as shown. Write the rules of usage under each punctuation mark.
4. Cut a large bone out of white construction paper. Use a bright marker to label the bone PUNCTUATION PUPS. Assemble the board as shown.

ART ACTIVITY:
Give each student a bone pattern. Have the students write a sentence on the bone for each punctuation mark. Display the bones on the bulletin board.

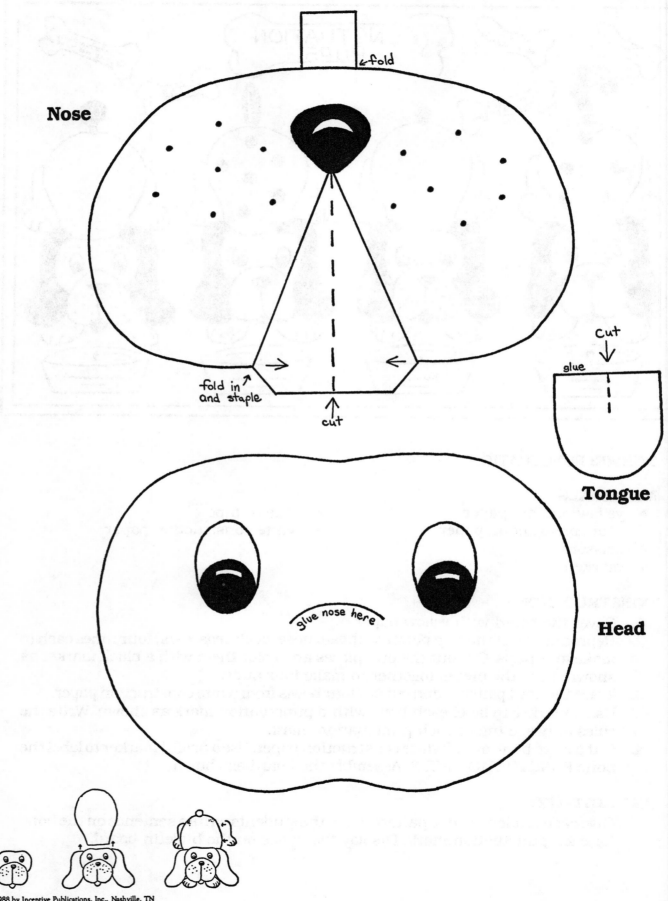

Nose

← fold

fold in
and staple

cut

Cut ↓

glue

Tongue

glue nose here

Head

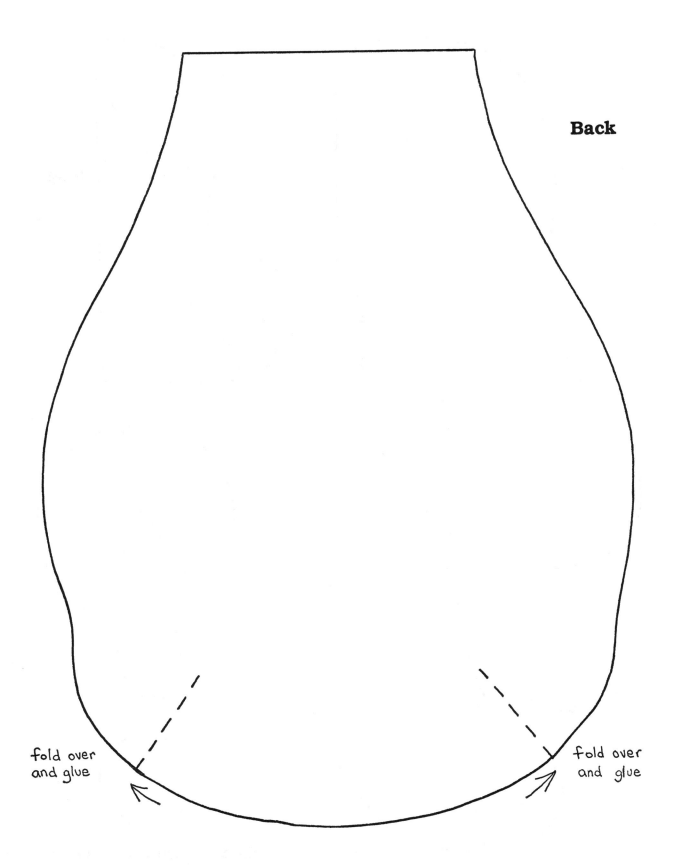

Back

fold over
and glue

fold over
and glue

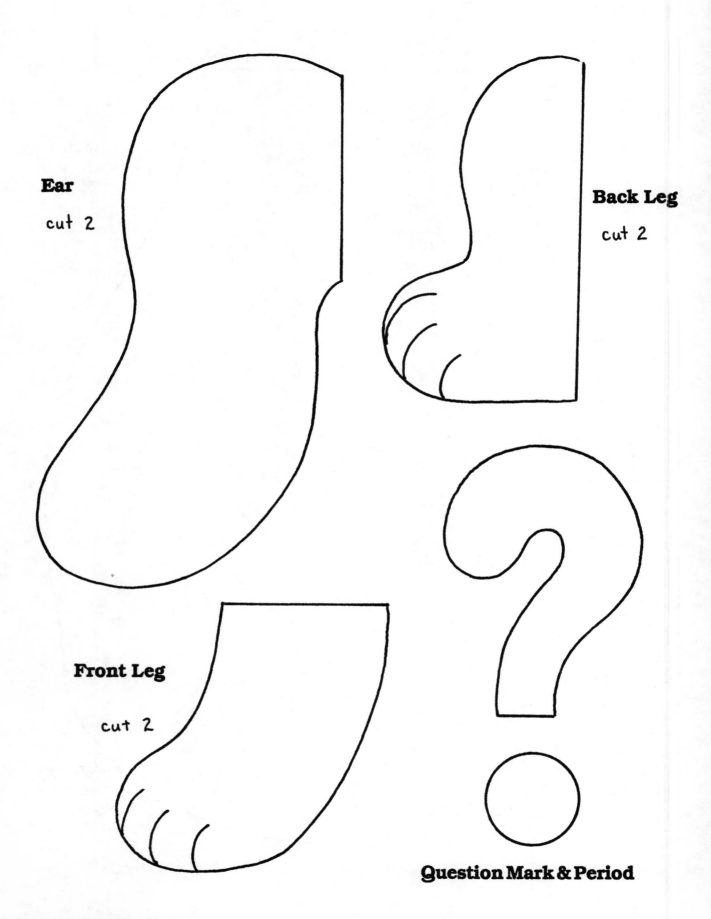

Ear

cut 2

Back Leg

cut 2

Front Leg

cut 2

Question Mark & Period

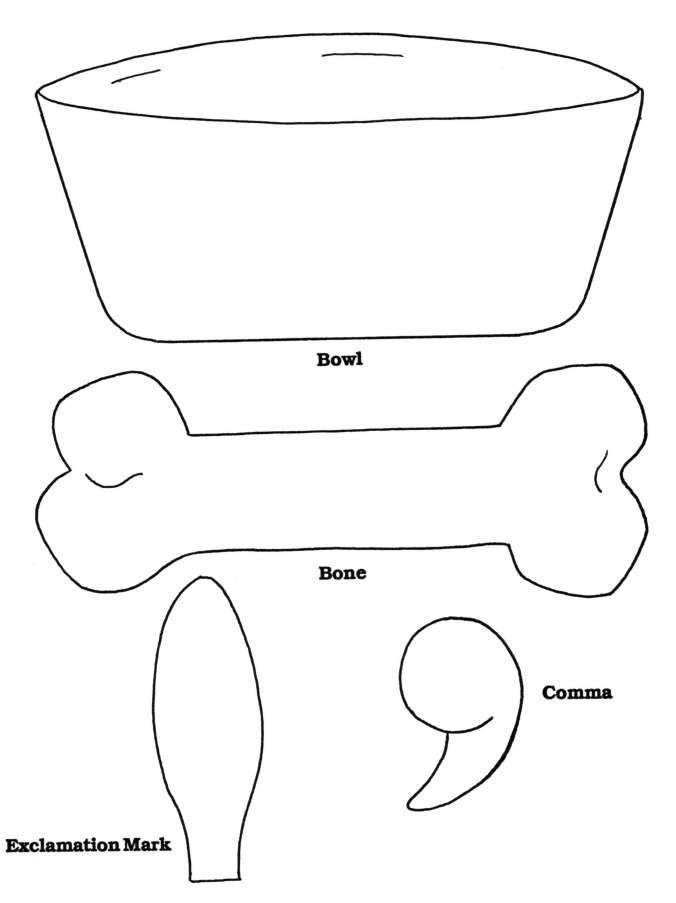

Bowl

Bone

Comma

Exclamation Mark

THEME: PARTS OF SPEECH

MATERIALS:
- yellow butcher paper or construction paper
- markers
- glue or tape
- paper bags
- construction paper (gray, blue, red)
- scissors

CONSTRUCTION:
1. Cover the board with yellow paper.
2. Trim the board in red.
3. Make a banner with blue construction paper. Cut letters to spell PARTS OF SPEECH out of red construction paper. Glue the letters to the banner.
4. Reproduce the patterns for the large elephant and color them accordingly.
5. Attach the banner, elephant, and seven paper bags to the board as shown. Label one bag "peanuts" and every other bag with a part of speech as shown.
6. Use the peanut pattern to make 30 to 50 peanuts. Write a word on each peanut that belongs in one of the parts of speech bags. Put the peanuts in the "peanut" bag.

ART ACTIVITY:
Have each student make a 3-D elephant using the small elephant patterns. Pin the elephants to the board as shown. Have each student pull a word from the peanut bag and place it in the proper parts of speech bag. Change the words weekly.

40

Head

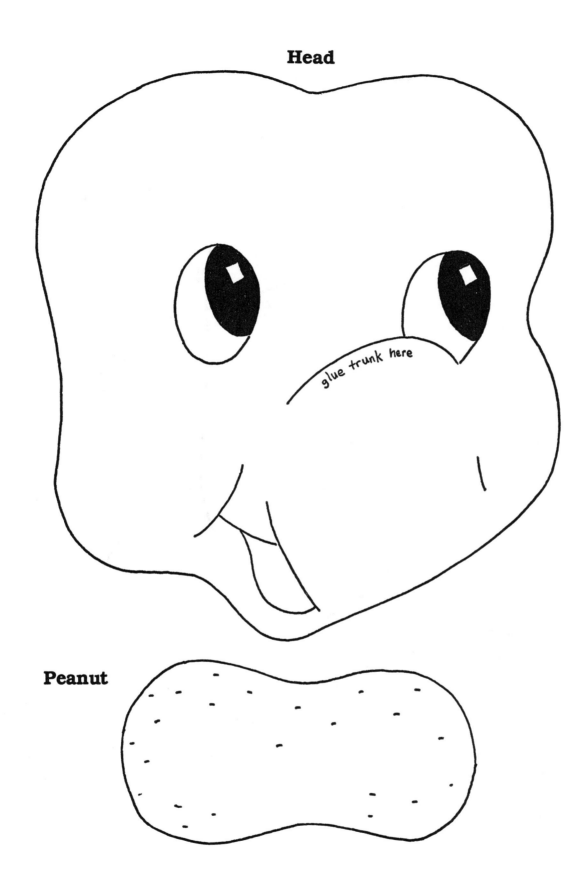

glue trunk here

Peanut

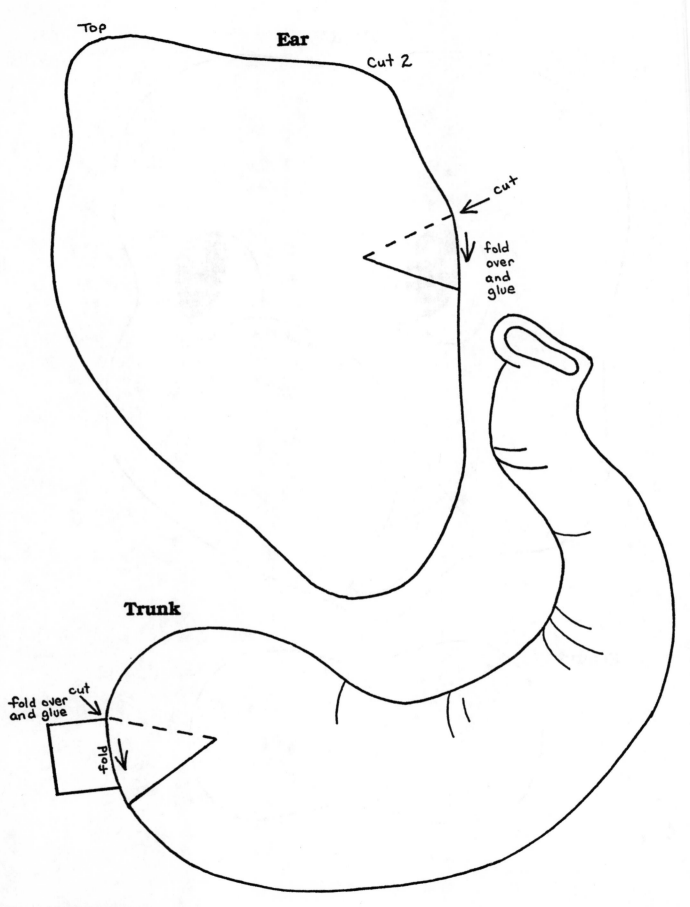

Top

Ear

Cut 2

cut

fold over and glue

Trunk

fold over and glue

cut

fold

Head

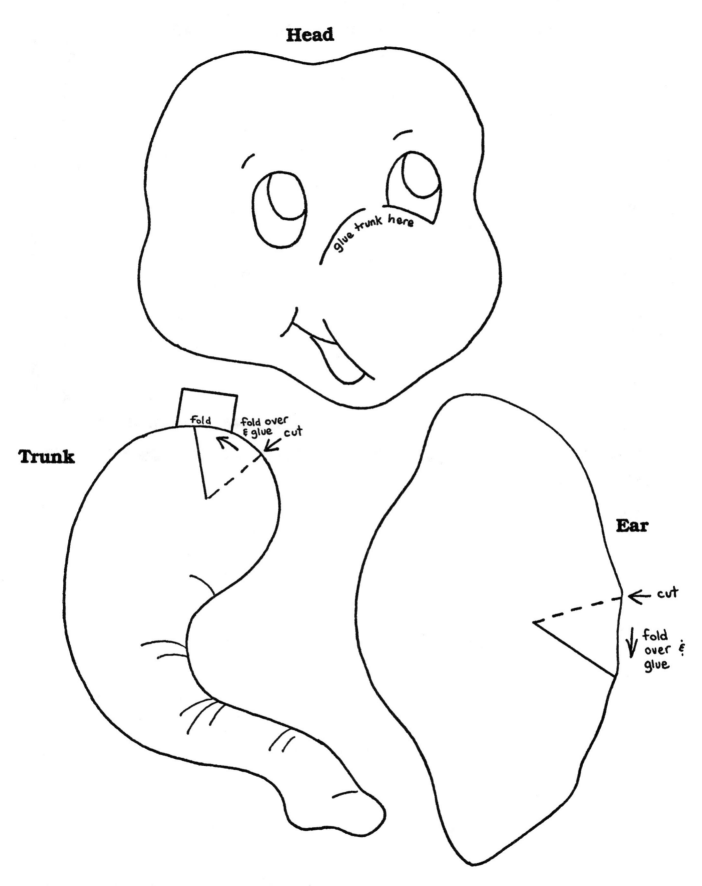

glue trunk here

Trunk

fold

fold over & glue

cut

Ear

← cut

↓ fold over & glue

Make a copy of this page for each student.

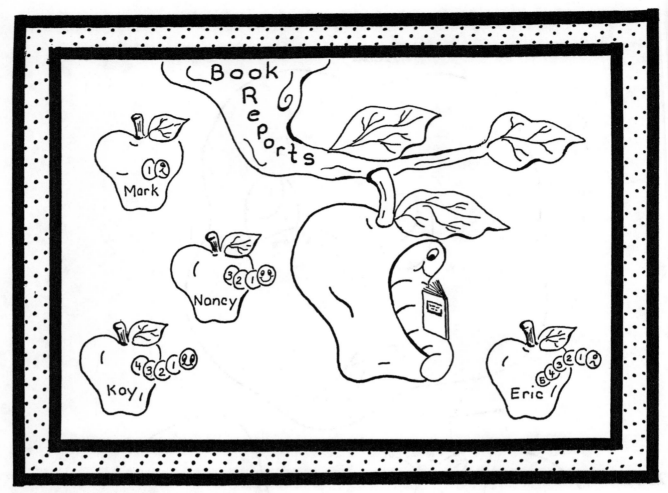

THEME: READING

MATERIALS:
- white butcher paper or construction paper
- glue or tape
- scissors
- crayons and markers
- construction paper (brown, red, green)

CONSTRUCTION:
1. Cover the board with white paper.
2. Trace the large apple pattern on red construction paper. Cut out the apple. Trace the worm pattern on green construction paper. Cut out the worm and glue it to the apple as shown. Cut out the book pattern and glue it to the worm.
3. Draw a branch on brown construction paper and cut it out (see illustration). Write BOOK REPORTS on the branch.
4. Assemble the board as shown in the illustration. Trim the bulletin board with a decorative border.

ART ACTIVITY:
Have each student cut out and color an apple and worm following the instructions on the pattern page. Each time a student reads a book or turns in a book report, let the student pull the worm out of the apple to show another section. Students may need to attach a small piece of tape to the back of the worm to make it secure. The students may compete with one another to see who can be the first to pull the worm all the way out of the apple!

44

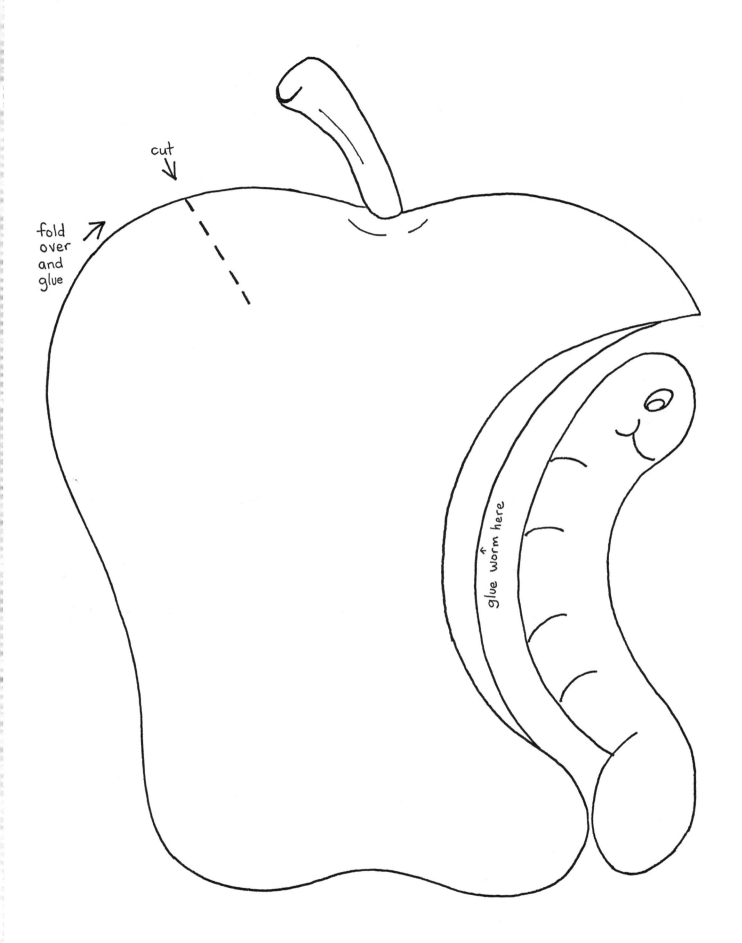

cut

fold
over
and
glue

glue worm here

1. Cut out the apple and worm and color them.
2. Draw a face on the worm and number each section.
3. Fold the worm like a fan.
4. Cut a slit in the apple as marked.
5. Insert the end of the worm through the slit and glue it in place.
6. Write your name on the apple.

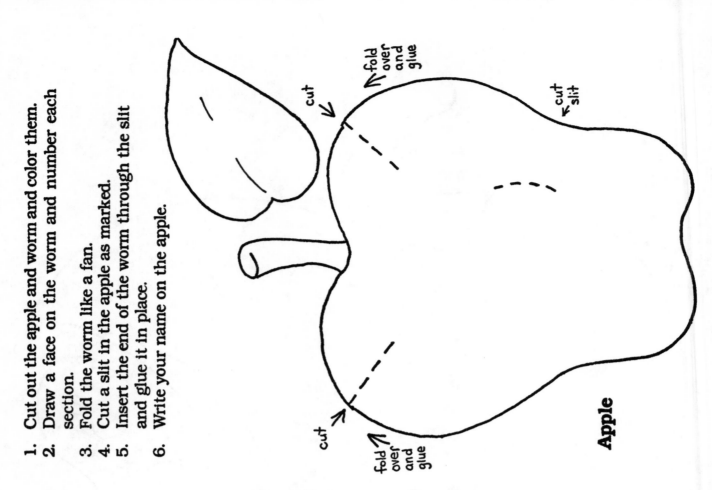

Apple

Make a copy of this page for each student.

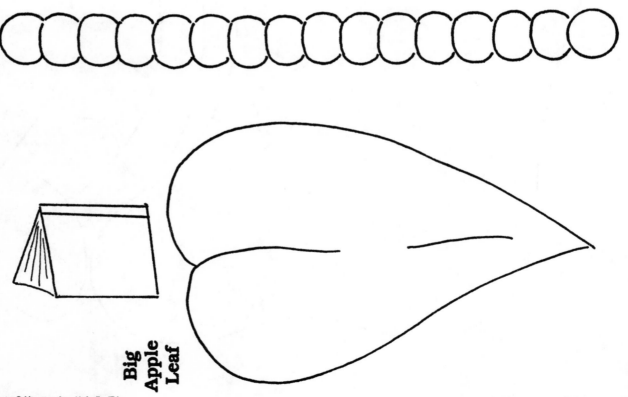

Big Apple Leaf

THEME: MATH SKILLS

MATERIALS:
- green butcher paper or construction paper
- brads
- crayons or markers
- construction paper (red, yellow, blue, black)
- glue or tape
- scissors

CONSTRUCTION:
1. Cover the board with green paper.
2. Reproduce both halves of the man pattern and color them accordingly.
3. Trace the two math machine strips on red construction paper. Cut out the strips. Use markers to decorate the u-shaped strip with numbers as shown in the illustration. Write MATH MACHINE across the top of the strip.
4. Use the provided pattern to cut two arrows out of black construction paper.
5. Cut two circles 8½" in diameter out of yellow construction paper. (These will be the large wheels of the machine.)
6. Use the small wheel pattern to cut two wheels out of blue construction paper. Follow the directions on the pattern page to put the wheels and the lower half of the machine together.
7. Assemble the board as shown.

ART ACTIVITY:
Have each student create a math machine of his or her own using the patterns and instructions provided.

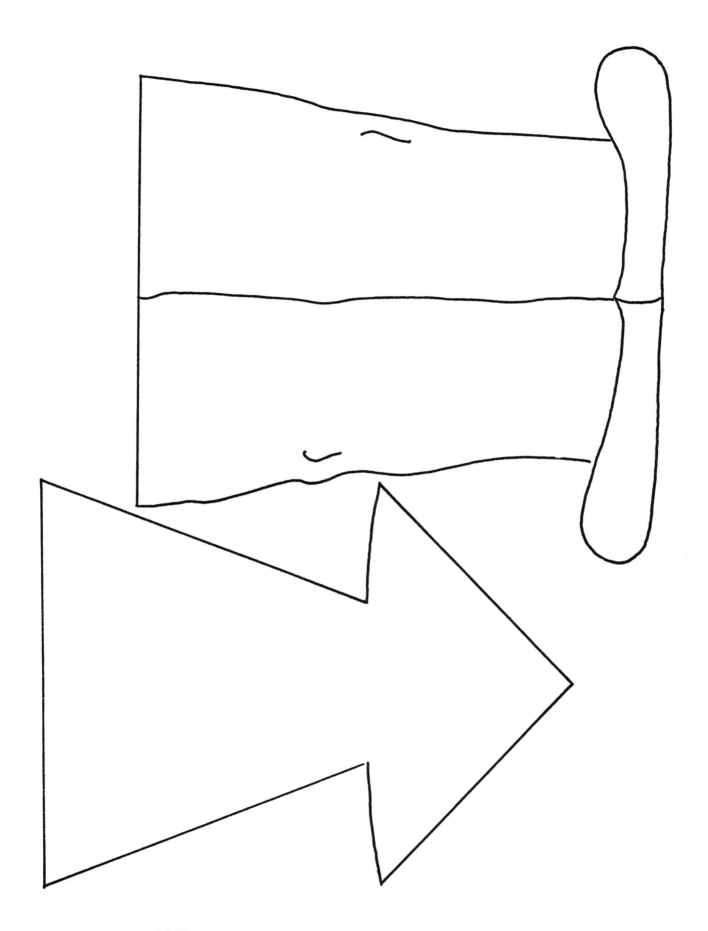

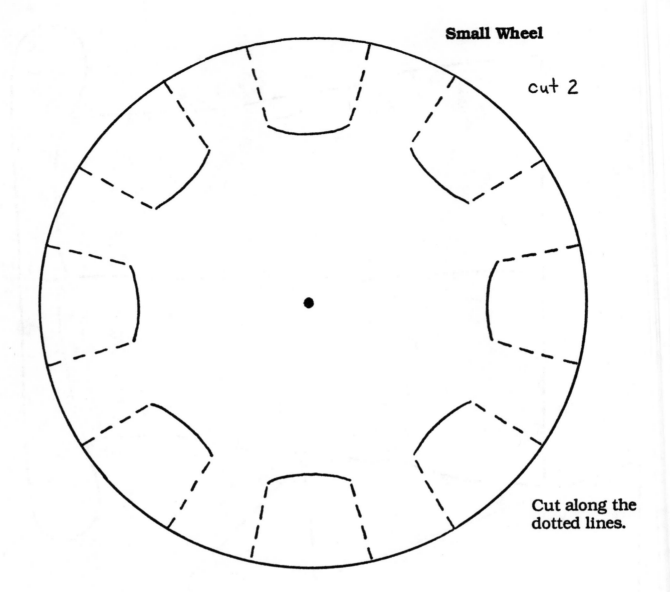

cut 2

Cut along the
dotted lines.

1. Glue the small wheel to the center of the large wheel. (Be careful not to glue the
    answer tabs.)
2. Insert a brad through the center of the wheels and attach a wheel to each side of
    the straight math machine strip.
3. Write math problems on the large wheels and the corresponding answers under
    the tabs.

Note: This is a self-check activity. Turn a problem on the wheel to the arrow and
then look behind the flap to check the answer.

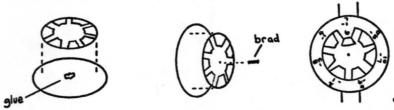

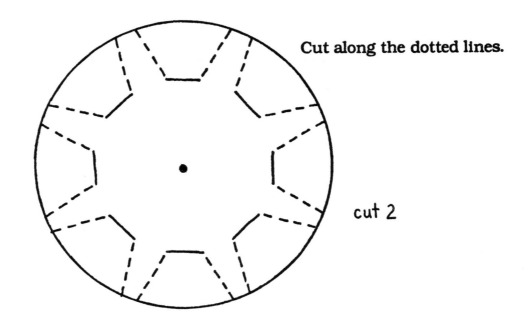

Cut along the dotted lines.

cut 2

Art Activity Patterns

Make a copy of this page for each student.

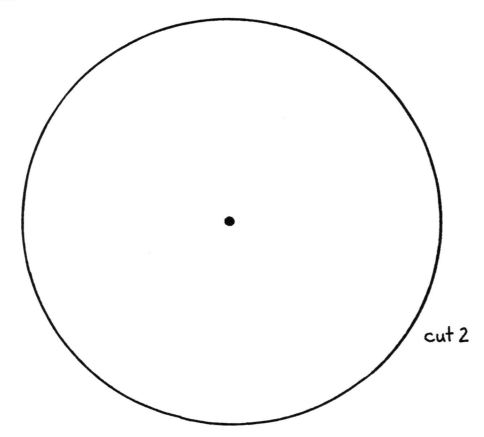

cut 2

1. Glue the small wheel to the center of the large wheel. (Be careful not to glue the answer tabs.)
2. Write math problems on the large wheel and the answers under the tabs.
3. Draw a math machine on a piece of construction paper (as on the bulletin board). Glue the wheels under the arrows. Turn a problem to the arrow and look behind the tab to check the answer.

put wheel here

↓
●

Cut out of
12" x 18"
construction
paper.

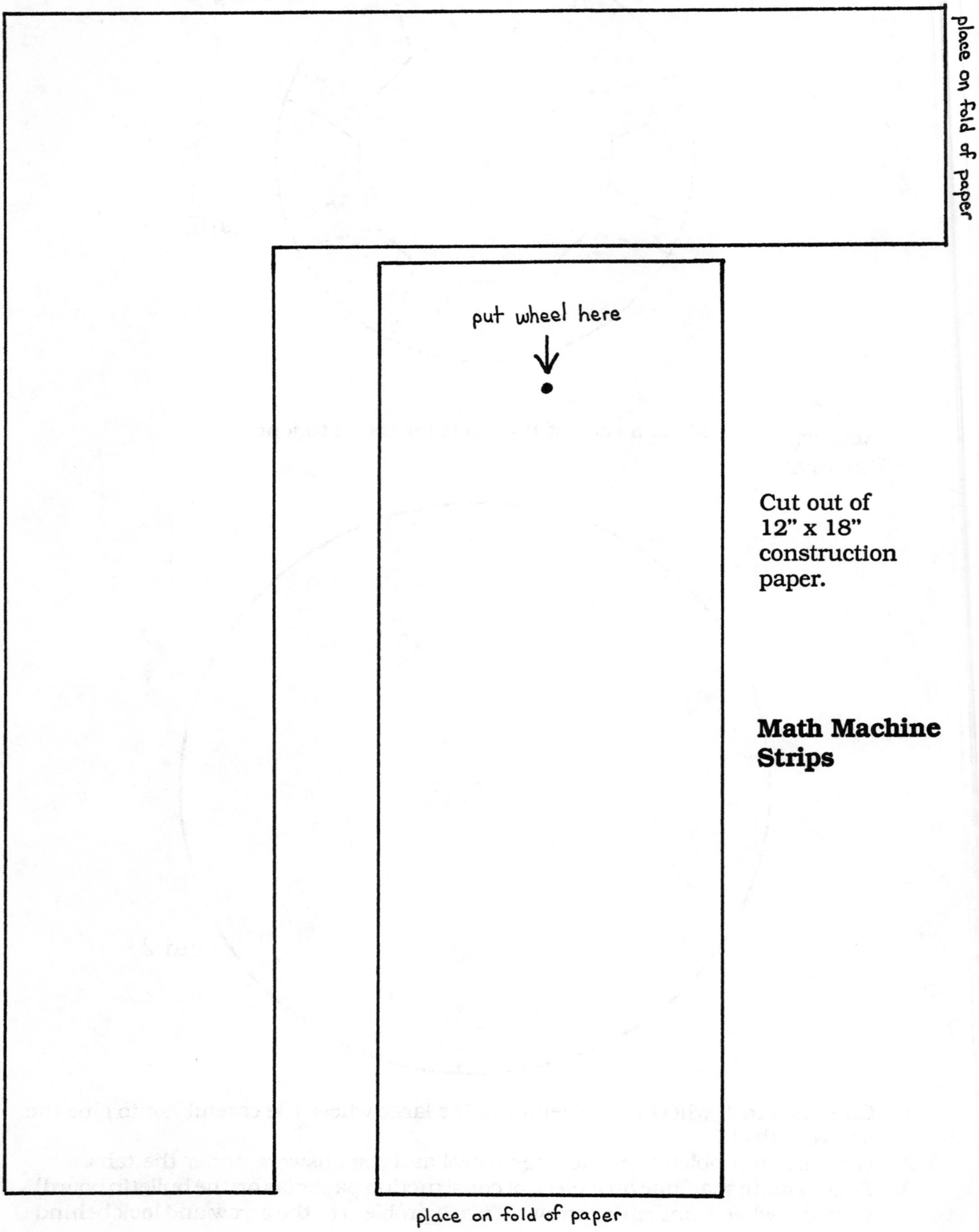

**Math Machine
Strips**

THEME: BACK TO SCHOOL

MATERIALS:
- blue butcher paper or construction paper
- scissors
- glue or tape
- construction paper (yellow, brown)
- crayons and markers

CONSTRUCTION:
1. Cover the board with blue paper.
2. Trace the large branch patterns on brown construction paper. Cut out the pieces and glue them together as marked to make a long branch.
3. Trace the moon pattern on yellow construction paper. Cut out the moon and draw an eye on the moon as shown.
4. Reproduce the large owl pattern and color the owl accordingly. Cut out the owl.
5. Glue or tape the moon, branch and owl to the bulletin board as shown in the illustration.
6. Use a marker to write the owl's "words" on the board as shown in the illustration. (Substitute your own name.)

ART ACTIVITY:
Let each student make a 3-D owl and a branch for the board using the patterns provided. Have the students write their names on the branches and color the owls.

Owl

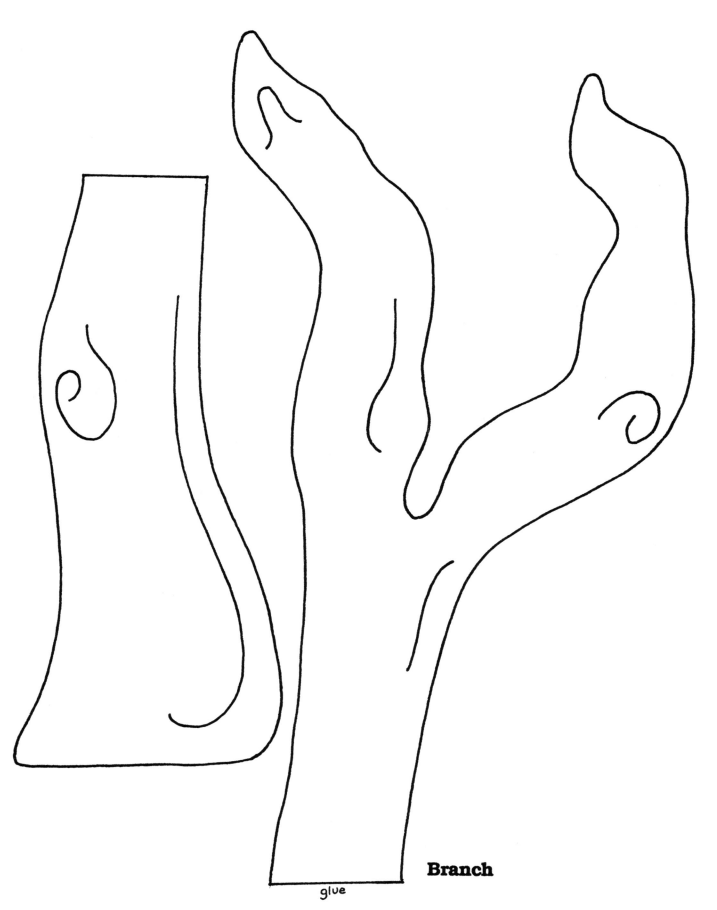

glue

Branch

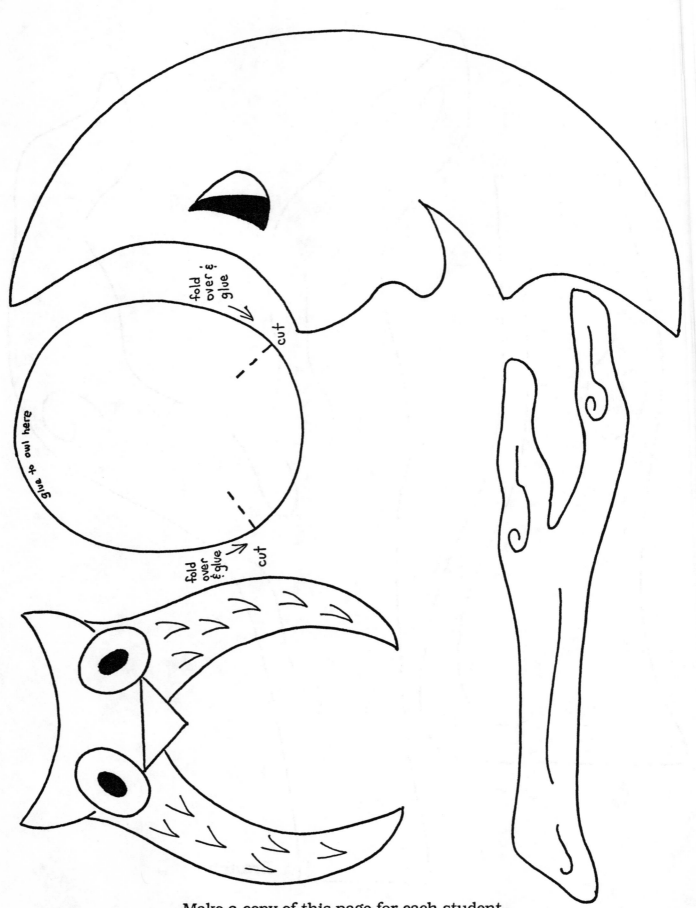

Text visible within the craft template:

fold over & glue

cut

glue to owl here

fold over & glue

cut

Make a copy of this page for each student.

THEME: FALL

MATERIALS:
- orange butcher paper or construction paper
- crayons
- scissors
- glue or tape
- construction paper (orange, brown, assorted colors)

CONSTRUCTION:
1. Cover the board with orange paper.
2. Cut out letters to spell FALL HARVEST from brown construction paper.
3. Trace the basket pattern on brown construction paper and then cut out the basket.
4. Trace the leaf and acorn patterns on assorted colors of construction paper. Cut out the patterns.
5. Using the illustration as a guide, glue or tape the letters and the basket (leaving the top "open") to the board. Attach the acorns and leaves around the board.

ART ACTIVITY:
Have each student make a 3-D fruit or vegetable using the patterns and instructions provided. The students may decorate their fruits and vegetables and then fill the basket!

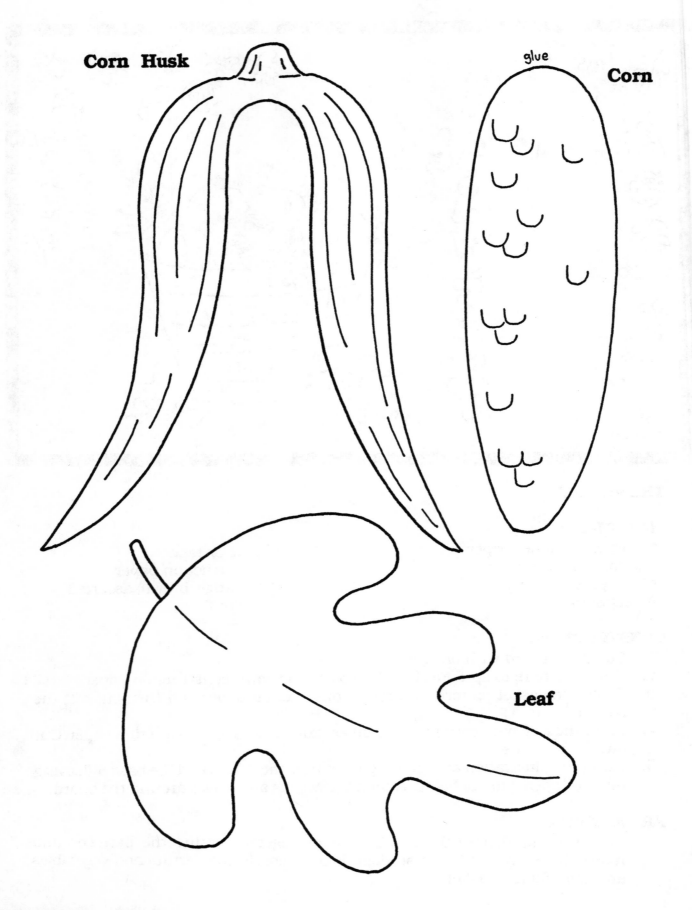

Corn Husk

Corn

glue

Leaf

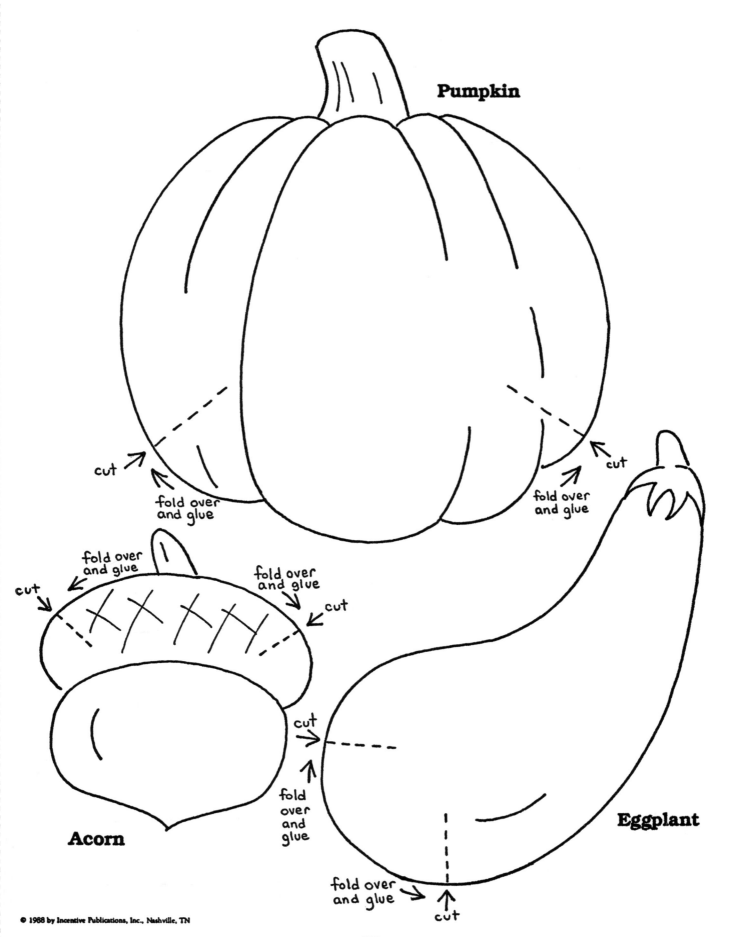

Pumpkin

cut

fold over
and glue

cut

fold over
and glue

fold over
and glue

cut

fold over
and glue

cut

Acorn

cut

fold
over
and
glue

Eggplant

fold over
and glue

cut

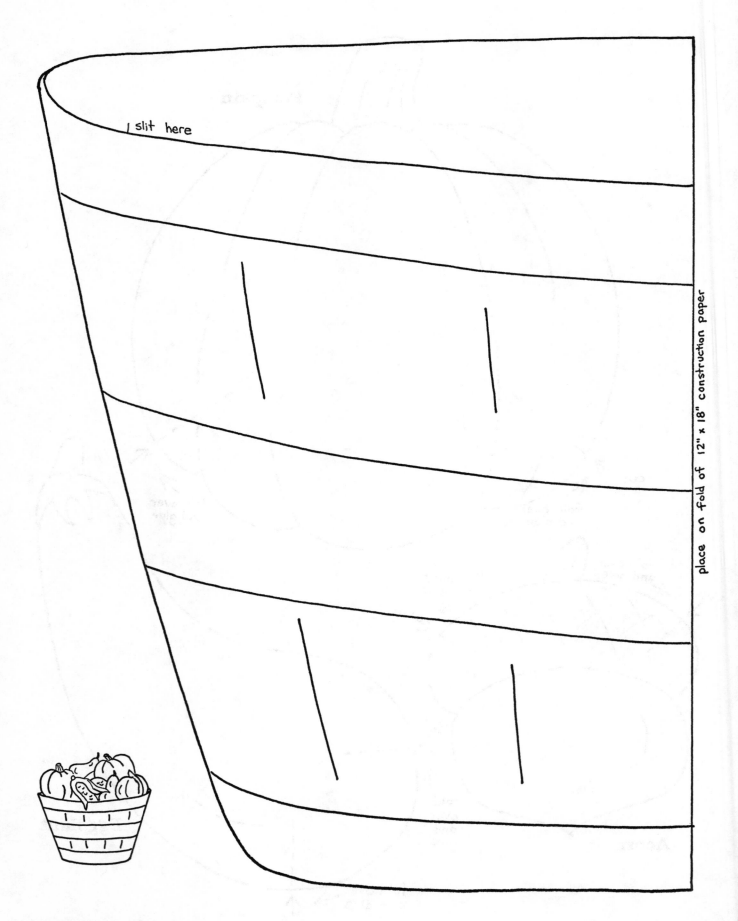

slit here

place on fold of 12" x 18" construction paper

THEME: HALLOWEEN

MATERIALS:
- orange butcher paper or construction paper
- white yarn
- 6" white pipe cleaners
- markers
- glue or tape
- scissors
- construction paper (black, white)

CONSTRUCTION:
1. Cover the board with orange paper.
2. Reproduce the witch patterns and color them accordingly.
3. Trace the kettle pattern on white construction paper and cut out the kettle. Color the brew purple, the flame orange, and the kettle black.
4. Make a sign out of white construction paper. Write HAPPY HALLOWEEN on the sign. Trim the board in black.
5. Attach the witch, kettle, and sign to the board as shown.

ART ACTIVITY:
Have each student make a 3-D spider web according to the instructions on the pattern page. Have the students make spiders for their webs. Hang the webs and spiders from the board with yarn.

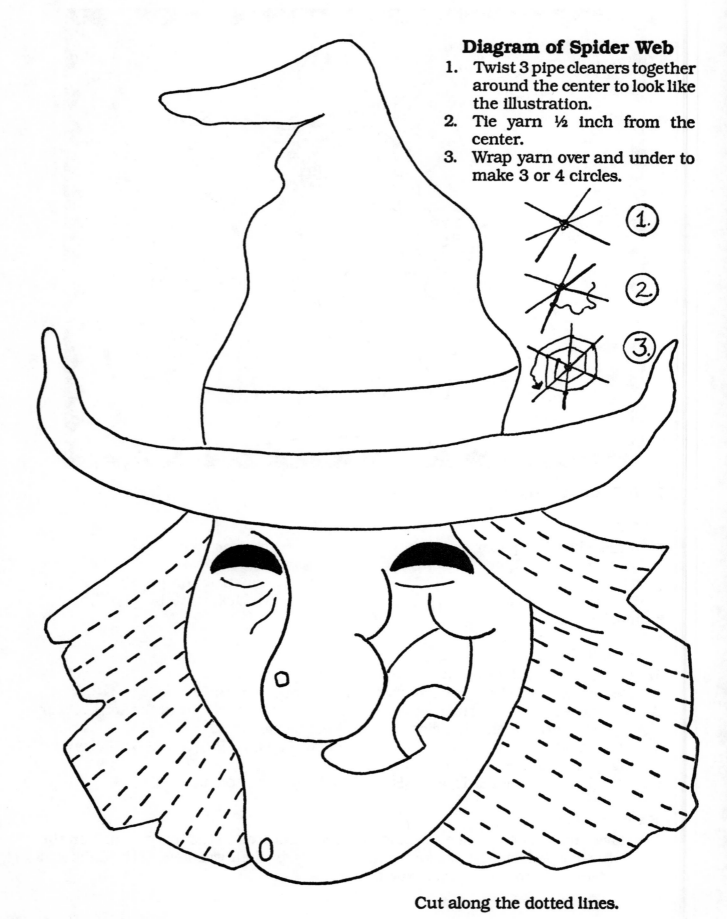

Diagram of Spider Web

1. Twist 3 pipe cleaners together around the center to look like the illustration.
2. Tie yarn ½ inch from the center.
3. Wrap yarn over and under to make 3 or 4 circles.

① ② ③

Cut along the dotted lines.

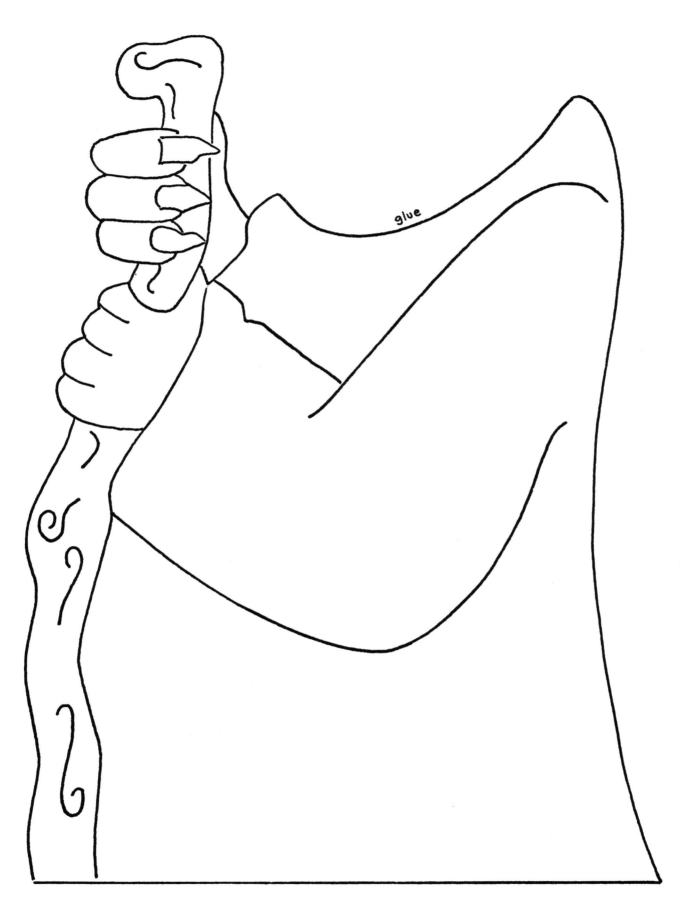

glue

place on fold of 12" x 18" construction paper

THEME: CHANUKAH

MATERIALS:
- blue or purple butcher paper or construction paper
- scissors
- marker
- glue or tape
- construction paper (yellow or gray)

CONSTRUCTION:
1. Cover the board with blue or purple paper.
2. Cut out the menorah patterns (candelabrum and base) and trace them on yellow or gray construction paper. Cut out the patterns and glue or tape them together.
3. Trace the candle pattern on construction paper to make eight candles.
4. Using the illustration as a guide, tape or glue the menorah and candles to the bulletin board. Use a marker to write "HAPPY CHANUKAH" on a banner made from blue or purple construction paper.

ART ACTIVITY:
Have each student make a 3-D Star of David for the bulletin board.

Star of David

1. Fold strip B to form a triangle and glue.
2. Cut the dotted lines on strip A.
3. Fold strip A to form a triangle and glue.
4. Insert strip A into strip B to form a star.

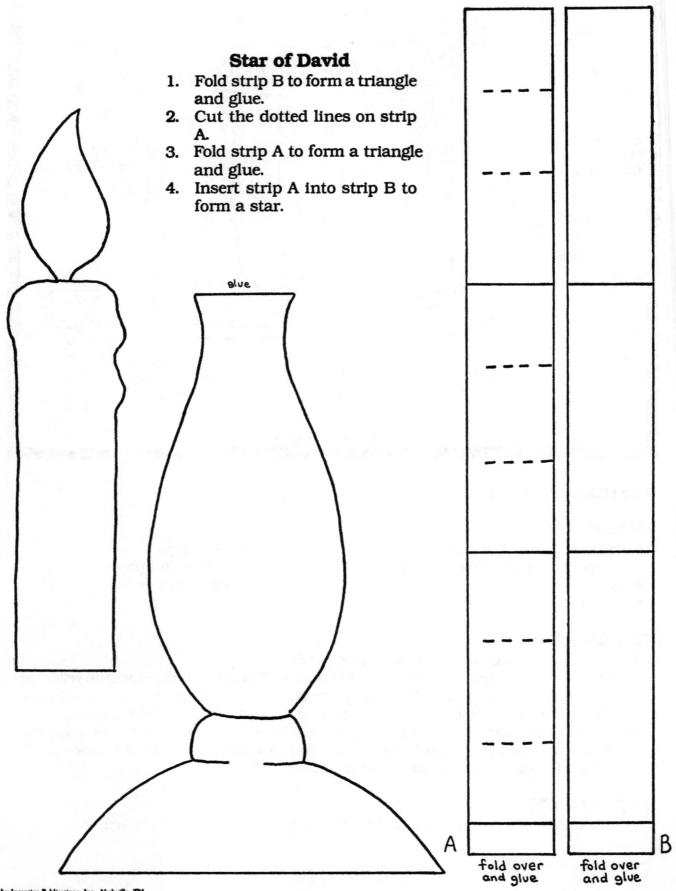

glue

A

B

fold over and glue

fold over and glue

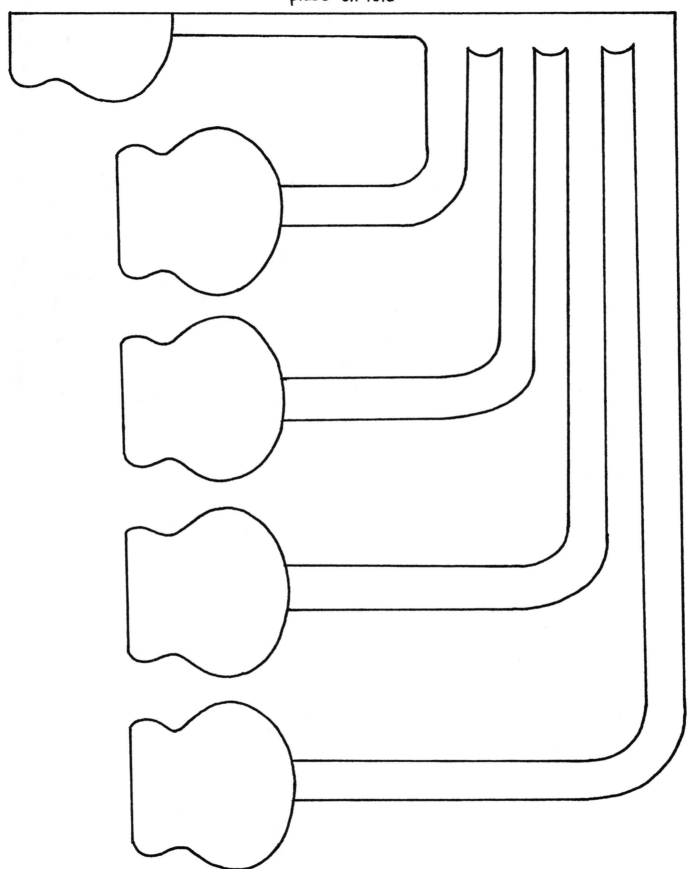

THEME: CHRISTMAS

MATERIALS:

- blue and white butcher paper
  or construction paper
- bathroom tissue tubes
- stapler
- scissors
- glue or tape
- markers
- construction paper
  (green, red, white)

CONSTRUCTION:

1. Cover the top 1/3 of the board with blue paper. Cover the bottom 2/3 of the board with white paper (see the illustration).
2. Trace the tree pattern on green construction paper to make two trees.
3. Trace and cut out enough holly to trim the corners of the board and the banner. Cut circles from red construction paper for berries.
4. Make a banner using white construction paper. Cut letters out of red construction paper to spell HAPPY HOLIDAYS and glue them on the banner.
5. Assemble the board as shown in the illustration.

ART ACTIVITY:

Have each student make a snowman by covering a bathroom tissue tube with white construction paper. Cut the top 1/3 off of the tube. Use this section for the snowman's head. Lay remaining section of the tube on its side and staple the head in the middle of the tube. The students can draw faces on the snowmen and add accessories such as hats, scarfs, and mittens. Pin the snowmen to the board.

place on fold of 12" x 18" construction paper

THEME: FEBRUARY

MATERIALS:
- yellow or light blue butcher paper or construction paper
- scissors
- stapler
- yarn
- markers
- glue or tape
- construction paper (black, white, red)

CONSTRUCTION:
1. Cover the board with yellow or light blue paper.
2. Trace both silhouette patterns on black construction paper. Cut out the silhouettes.
3. Trace the dove and banner patterns on white construction paper. Cut out the patterns. Label one banner with Lincoln's name and birth date, and one with Washington's name and birth date.
4. Cut letters out of red construction paper to spell FEBRUARY.
5. Assemble the board as shown in the illustration.

ART ACTIVITY:
Have each student make a 3-D valentine using the pattern and directions provided. Let each student hang a valentine on the board.

Lincoln

Washington

cut 2

1. Cut out two hearts.
2. Place the hearts together and glue them together at the top, center, and bottom.
3. Fold the sides out to make a 3-D heart.
4. Decorate all four sides with crayons or markers.
5. Tie a piece of yarn through both hearts to hang the 3-D valentine on the bulletin board.

Make a copy of this page for each student.

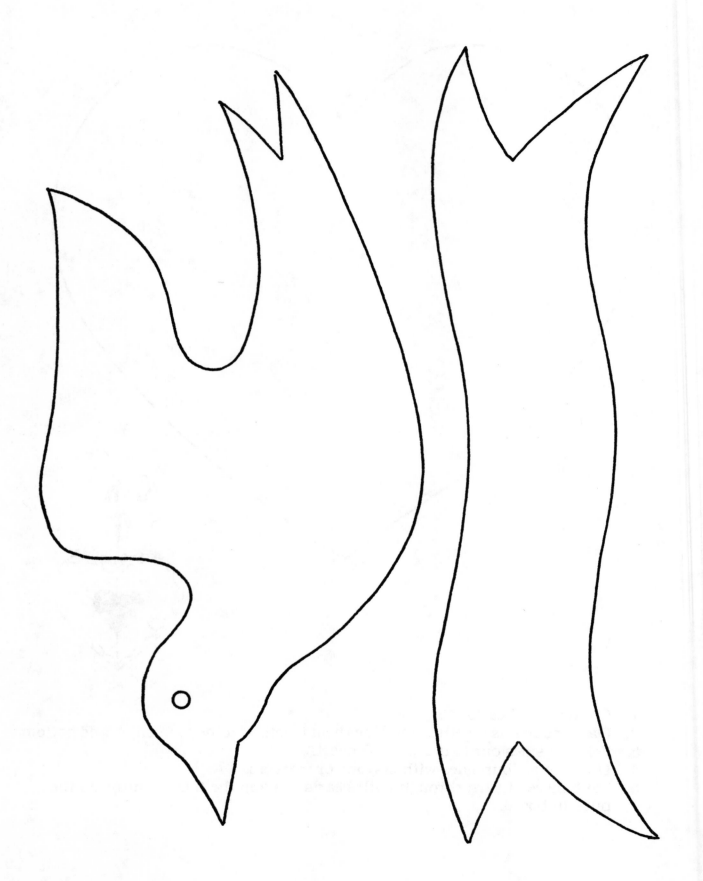

THEME: EASTER

MATERIALS:
- construction paper (pink, purple, yellow)
- pipe cleaners for flower stems
- glue or tape
- green butcher paper or construction paper
- scissors

CONSTRUCTION:
1. Cover the board with green paper.
2. Trim the board in yellow.
3. Cut letters out of purple construction paper to spell HAPPY EASTER.
4. Use the egg pattern to cut an egg out of pink, purple, and yellow construction paper.
5. Trace the chick pattern on yellow construction paper. Cut out the chick and tape or glue it to the cracked egg.

ART ACTIVITY:
Have the students make spring flowers for the bulletin board using the patterns and instructions on the pattern page. Curl the leaves around a pencil to add dimension.

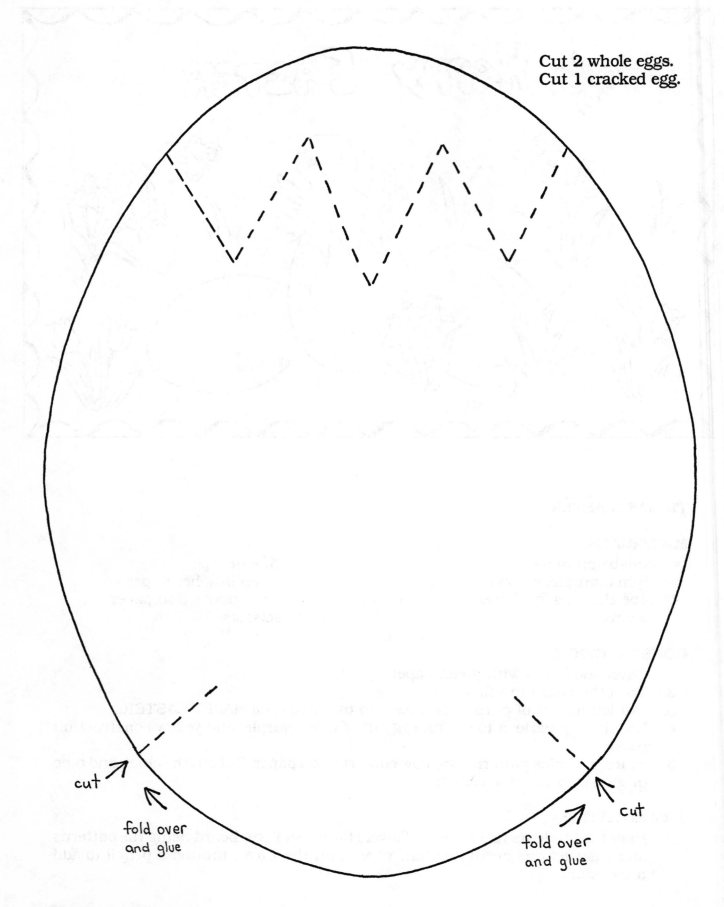

Cut 2 whole eggs.
Cut 1 cracked egg.

cut

fold over
and glue

cut

fold over
and glue

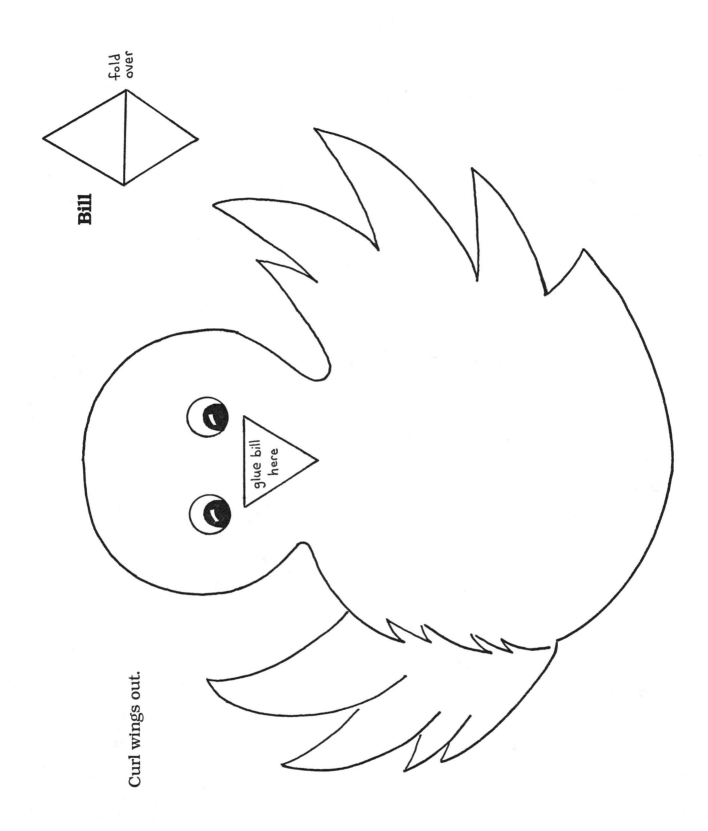

Bill

fold over

glue bill here

Curl wings out.

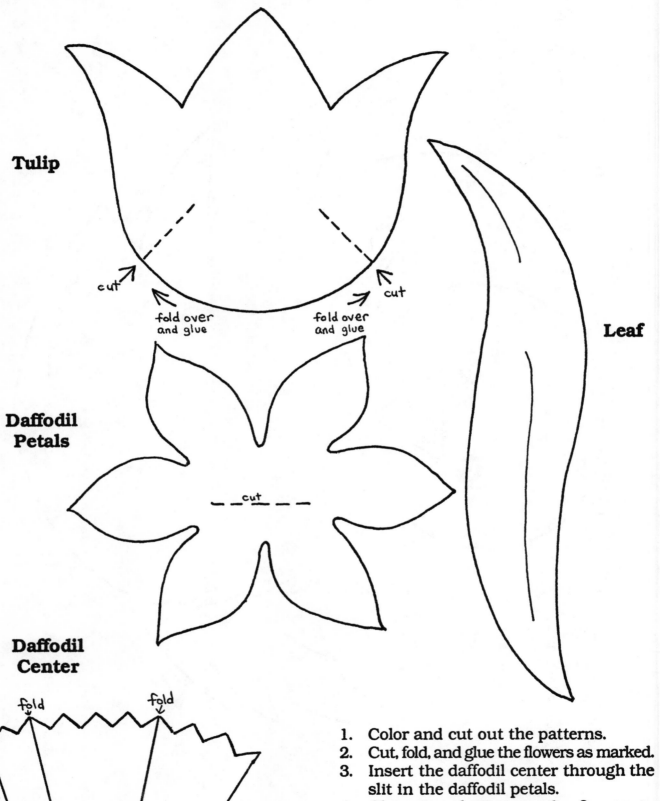

Tulip

cut

fold over
and glue

fold over
and glue

cut

Leaf

**Daffodil
Petals**

cut

**Daffodil
Center**

fold

fold

glue

glue

glue

glue

1. Color and cut out the patterns.
2. Cut, fold, and glue the flowers as marked.
3. Insert the daffodil center through the slit in the daffodil petals.
4. Glue pipe cleaners to the flowers to make stems.
5. Glue several leaves on the pipe cleaner stems.